LEADERSHIP
to WIN

LEADERSHIP
to WIN

A Biography of R. Clayton McWhorter

BOB VRACIU

Hillsboro Press

PROVIDENCE PUBLISHING CORPORATION

FRANKLIN, TENNESSEE

Printed in the United States of America

07   06   05   04   03   1   2   3   4   5

Library of Congress Catalog Card Number: 2003111214

ISBN: 1-57736-301-9

Cover photo by Micael-Reneé Lifestyle Portraiture
Cover design by John Tracy

HILLSBORO PRESS
an imprint of
Providence Publishing Corporation
238 Seaboard Lane • Franklin, Tennessee 37067
www.providence-publishing.com

To those who dream big and dream often;
To those who see business, life, and community as inexplicitly intertwined;
To those who truly care about helping others and make the effort to do so,
The story told in this book is about a kindred spirit . . . enjoy!

Contents

People who know R. Clayton McWhorter wouldn't be surprised if his tombstone read: "I was blessed beyond my wildest dreams . . . I tried to make a difference and *I did*!" Hopefully it will be many years before an epitaph is necessary and he will have made a difference in the lives of many more people.

His story is inspirational and provides a roadmap for others to follow. It is a good story about a very successful business man. It a good story about personal triumph for a young man who was able to climb out of poverty and establish himself not only as a successful professional, but also a role model for so many people. But there are many such "rags-to-riches" stories, and some describe conquests and riches that eclipse those of Clayton's career. What makes it such an exceptional story is the way these accomplishments were achieved. It is a story about:

- How a mother (a single parent for many years) fought for her four children's futures and instilled in them a set of values that not only served them well, but benefitted the communities within which they lived.

- How mentors can play important roles in shaping the fabric of a person's personal and professional lives.

- How the successful seven-year life of HealthTrust, Inc. created a venue for many good business practices that became lessons for others in business.

- How an accomplished business executive can build a management team by seeking out people who are smarter than he is and getting results through them.

- How a successful businessman can balance the demands of running a business with a passion for "giving back" to the community that allowed that business to be successful, and who truly believes that "you will be rewarded for giving back and serving others."

- An exception to the common phrase, "nice guys finish last." This is a man who is genuinely humble, interested in others, knows how to make people around him feel comfortable and special, and is always guided by the principle of "doing the right thing." Far from finishing last, he is in an elite group who are leading the pack.

Chapter one describes Clayton's early personal life through the metamorphous where he evolved from being a pharmacist to becoming president of Hospital Corporation of America (HCA), the largest health-care company in the world.

Chapter two tells the HealthTrust story; how the $2.1 billion spin-off from HCA had a remarkable eight-year run and how Clayton, as CEO, was able to further develop his leadership abilities.

Chapter three is a description of the short period Clayton served as chairman of the board of Columbia/HCA following Columbia/HCA's acquisition of HealthTrust in 1995. This period in his life helped delineate the "first half" of his professional life from the "second half."

Chapter four describes the focus of the first five years of his "second half." During this time, he created Clayton Associates, a venture capital firm, and pursued two of his passions: "giving back" and "making a difference in the lives of others." How Clayton has pursued these passions and the results are inspirational and exemplary.

Chapter five presents some principles and lessons that can be gleaned from analyzing Clayton's approach to business, people, and life—an approach which doesn't distinguish between the three. Additionally, chapter five describes the highly unusual relationship between Clayton and one of his mentors—Owen Brackett (O. B.) Hardy.

Interestingly, some of the advice O. B. provided to Clayton (and included in this chapter) is sound advice to anyone navigating the difficult waters of the business world.

This book was written by someone who has worked with Clayton for over twenty years and considers himself a big fan. It was truly a labor of love—my chance to give something back to a person who has provided me with so much.

In writing this book, I had tacit approval to "tell things the way they are." So part of Clayton's story includes episodes and stories that make his journey all the more believable. Not everything worked out, and even the man once dubbed "The Godfather of Nashville health care" made mistakes.

As the material for this book was pulled together, many people shared their views and perspectives in the form of letters and interviews. The author is truly appreciative for these contributions. It seems like so many people who have been touched by Clayton wanted to "give back" a little of what they have received.

An undertaking of this nature can't help but impinge upon other priorities. My wife, Jeannie, deserves special mention for her understanding and support during the many hours I spent in "my cave." We both know it was for the right reasons!

Bob Vraciu
Brentwood, Tennessee
March 2003

LEADERSHIP
to WIN

Chapter One

RALPH CLAYTON MCWHORTER
THE MAKING OF THE MAN

Like so many people who have enjoyed success in life, Clayton's early years laid the groundwork for that success. Perhaps it is the hardships of one's early years that creates the drive and instills the values necessary to succeed. Certainly Clayton's childhood supports this notion.

TRAUMAS AND THE HARD LIFE

Ralph Clayton McWhorter was born on September 27, 1933, in Chattanooga, Tennessee. He was the fourth child of Gladys and Ralph Clayton McWhorter Sr. For the man who had so much success in the hospital industry, his parents couldn't afford a hospital delivery and he was born at home. The family stories claim he was born on the kitchen table, but Clayton claims to have been "too young to remember." Whether the delivery was on the kitchen table or in a bed, it didn't matter . . . the McWhorter family didn't have much money.

When Clayton was two years old, his parents separated and later divorced. Gladys McWhorter moved herself and the four children to Lafayette, Georgia, about thirty miles south of Chattanooga. The small farmhouse the family occupied reflected the family's economic status. There was no electricity, indoor plumbing, or locks on the exterior doors. Nighttime reading was done with light from kerosene lamps. The family's income came largely from Gladys who worked at the Peerless Woolen Mill in Rossville, Georgia. The family also sharecropped the farm with another family. Clayton and his siblings did much of the farmwork raising corn and cotton.

After four years, the family moved into a larger, three-bedroom farmhouse nearby. They renovated the house and Clayton tells the story about a bedroom addition onto the back of the house. A wall made out of "slabs" encased the concrete floor. Slabs are the throwaway cuttings when lumber is cut from a tree trunk . . . the bark side faced out. The inside of the wall was covered with tarpaper. Since the potbelly heater in the main part of the house could not effectively heat this bedroom, many blankets were used on cold winter nights.

Clayton still remembers how it felt to be poor. During this period, Christmas gifts were limited to what Peerless gave their employees. Gladys couldn't afford to buy anything else. One year Clayton got a bow and arrow set that was provided by Peerless. When he and his brothers strung the bow, it broke, so Clayton thought, *there goes Christmas for me*. His brothers carved a replacement out of a hickory branch. So Christmas was salvaged, but it was still lean. And almost sixty years later, he can recall the "high" from the simple gift, the feeling of loss when the bow was broken, and the appreciation for his brothers who carved a substitute.

As the family struggled financially, Clayton recalls some of the early lessons that helped shape his character. First was the work discipline enforced by his oldest brother, Wayne. The farmwork was handled largely by Clayton and his two brothers.

> My older brother Wayne was the "straw boss." He would plow the field for corn and Fred and I would hoe the field to rid it of weeds. Anytime we leaned on the hoe, Wayne was quick to yell at us. Anytime he was leaning on the plow, he was "resting the mule." But looking back, it was a good thing that he taught us some discipline. Otherwise, we might have leaned on the hoes all day long.

The young Clayton had developed a quick temper and was prone to "slug it out with others." His third grade teacher, Ms. Cramer, taught him to count to ten before he did something while he was angry. She said, "If you don't, you will never make it in this world." He found it

*Left: Gladys McWhorter. **Right:** Clayton in a high school picture.*

easier said than done. But, through the years, he not only did the counting as taught, but learned to take short walks when there were decisions to be made in the face of anger.

The next big change came when Clayton was ready to enter junior high school. His mother remarried and the family relocated to Chattanooga, Tennessee. His stepfather was George Edson who worked with Gladys at the Peerless Woolen Mill. George had a house in Chattanooga, and the McWhorter children thought they had "died and gone to heaven" because it was a "real house" in the "big city."

While the move and suddenly having a stepfather was a big change, it was Clayton's enrollment in Brainerd Junior High School that proved to be the big shock. Simply stated, he was not prepared. His previous school experience failed to give him the study habits and grounding necessary to do well in the new school. Clayton had previously attended Bethel School which consisted of a one-room building with seven grades. His class in Bethel School had two other students and he wasn't challenged. As he struggled at Brainerd, his mother pushed him, and eventually he was able to earn better grades.

The life in Chattanooga was short-lived. Two years after the move, George Edson accepted a job with another woolen mill in Vermont and went ahead to begin the job. On the day their belongings had been loaded on the moving van, they received word that George had suffered a heart attack and died. So, the family instantly went from being on the brink of moving to Vermont with all the excitement and fears such a move brings, to having to bury their stepfather/husband and find a place to live. Their house in Chattanooga had already been sold.

They moved into a two-bedroom house in Fairview, located in northeast Georgia, not far from the Peerless Woolen Mill in Rossville. Clayton lived there until he graduated from high school. While their housing had improved from their previous home in Lafayette, money was still tight.

During Clayton's senior year in high school, his mother remarried. His new stepfather was Carter Franks. Carter was a fireman who also had a wallpaper hanging business during his off time. During the summer months, Clayton helped hang wallpaper. His job was to apply the paste to the wall and Carter hung the paper. To this day, Clayton is still amazed at how often Carter had to slow down to wait for him. After Clayton's senior year, Gladys and Carter moved to a suburb of Chattanooga, East Lake, where they lived for over thirty years until death claimed them. East Lake was Clayton's summer home while in college.

THE FAMILY INFLUENCE

Gladys and her first husband, Ralph, had three children before Clayton was born as their youngest. Wayne was six years older, Fred was four years older, and Bernice was two years older than Clayton. Each of his siblings played a role in shaping Clayton's character and personality.

Wayne, the oldest, set the academic standard by which both Clayton and Fred were judged. Clayton describes Wayne as brilliant—someone who always had "the answer." Because school and grades always came easily to him, the other siblings were expected to do as well, or at least that is what they were told. Wayne graduated at the top of his class in high school, and the little time he spent in the classroom was generally spent taking tests. He went on to Georgia Tech to study chemical engineering and subsequently became an expert in resins and paints. He also displayed practical skills like the ability to take radios and televisions apart and then reassemble them in working order.

Wayne was blessed with a photographic memory, something not shared by his siblings. Clayton recalls one of the demonstrations. While Clayton was studying to become a pharmacist, he brought home *Remington's Practice of Pharmacy*, the gold standard for running a pharmacy. Wayne challenged Clayton to show him the most difficult chapter. After spending about fifteen minutes reading the chapter, he told Clayton, "Ask me any question." After several attempts to trip-up Wayne, Clayton had to give up because he had learned the chapter. This story just illustrates part of Wayne's influence on the young Clayton. As the leader among the children, he created expectations of academic performance for which the other siblings were held accountable. Gladys McWhorter would frequently try to motivate the other children by saying, "If Wayne can do it, then you certainly can do it."

Fred McWhorter was closer in age to Clayton, being only four years older. This created more opportunities for the two to develop a strong relationship and fight ("a lot"). There is the appearance that Clayton followed in Fred's footsteps and both feel a strong bond, even to this day. Clayton describes the young Fred as athletic, smart in a practical sense, and "strong as an ox." Both Fred and Clayton had to work harder in school than Wayne, and it is no coincidence that both brothers graduated and worked as pharmacists. Perhaps in some sense, Fred was a role model for Clayton, filling part of the void when there was no father figure at home.

Bernice feels like she played a significant role in raising Clayton, even though she was only two years older. She had to fill in for their mother while Gladys was away at work. She had the indoor jobs (cooking, cleaning, etc.) while the boys had the outdoor jobs. Clayton recalls, "She was really the glue that kept the family operating. She was 'tough as nails' and, even though we brothers had our differences, we

The McWhorter siblings in 1961: Wayne, Fred, Bernice, and Clayton.

had the love and respect for her." She developed into a woman much like her mother, even to the point that in looks, mannerisms, work ethic, nurturing nature, and the way she would feed Clayton in later years when he traveled through Chattanooga . . . she had in essence become her mother.

Clayton's admiration for her grew even more when she took care of their mother during the last years of Gladys's life. "It is one thing to financially support someone; it is another to give of your time, love, and attention. Bernice was there when Mother needed the help."

Bernice not only protected the young Clayton, but found ways to coerce him into doing what she wanted him to do. For example, she caught Clayton smoking while he was in junior high school. Rather than tell their mother, she convinced Clayton to help her with some of her chores. Thus Gladys saw Clayton cleaning dishes, pots, and pans, and was amazed that Clayton was so willing to help his sister.

While Clayton's three siblings all played some role in shaping his character, it was his mother who was the most important person in his early life. Clayton describes her as a "special lady who was tough as nails, but taught us some valuable lessons . . . taught us a value system." During many of Clayton's formative years, she had to raise the four children by herself and did so with a firm hand. That firm hand administered a few whippings, but she more frequently resorted to *the lecture* as a way of expressing her displeasure. It went something like this: "Young man, do you know what you are doing to your poor ole mother? You are sending her to an early grave. I can't believe you did what you did . . ." By this point, Clayton would think, *Just whip me and get it over with.* This method of criticism and guilt-tripping was very effective; the children didn't want to disappoint her. Of course, they still got into trouble, so the lecture was repeated often.

What is apparent in Clayton's life, even today, is a set of values that he attributes to his mother. These include:

- Be Honest
- Give Back
- Be Proud
- Be Respectful
- Work Hard
- Be Frugal
- Support the Church
- "You Can Be Whatever You Want To Be"

Gladys McWhorter not only instilled these values in her children, but she lived them in her own life. When the family lived in the small farmhouse in Lafayette, Georgia, Gladys had to walk three miles to catch a ride with a coworker to the Peerless Woolen Mill, which was twenty-five miles away. She made this trip five or six days per week, whether she was sick or well, and in good weather or bad, and she never complained. She worked hard and expected her children to work hard as well. They had chores and part-time jobs throughout their school years.

For Clayton, this strong work ethic led to his working some sort of job as far back as he can remember whether it was farmwork or cutting grass. When he was old enough, he sought part-time employment. A few examples of his high school jobs illustrate part of his education by hard knocks. Clayton delivered morning papers to homes using an old army bicycle. The way people treated the paperboy when it was time for him to collect subscription payments was a quick education about deceit and avoidance. Lots of excuses such as: 1) People would offer to pay with a fifty-dollar bill, knowing it would be nearly impossible for Clayton to have enough change; 2) Sometimes people would not answer the door even though they were at home; and 3) People would tell Clayton to come back because someone else would have to pay him.

During high school, he worked in the meat department of a local grocery store during the afternoons and on Saturdays. One lesson learned was about the harmful effects of alcoholism. "The store owner would go on a drinking binge and would be gone for a week or ten days, so his wife would have to come into the store. I got thrown into some decision-making at a young age, and I saw how disruptive the owner's behavior was to his family. I hoped it would never happen to me."

During his senior year, Clayton worked at a dry cleaning store in the mornings until school opened. After school he worked at L. C. Longley Pharmacy. This made for some long days, especially given his mother's requirement for doing well in school. Clayton gives three reasons that he worked so hard. First, he needed to earn and save money for college. Second, his brothers and sister had set a standard, working hard as well. It wasn't even a question for the fourth born. And lastly, "We each had to prove something for ourselves. My mother pushed us to prove we could be whatever we wanted to be. Hard work was the only way that was going to happen."

Besides pushing a strong work ethic, Gladys taught other lessons. Clayton tells one story about how he received a whipping because his mother thought he was not telling the truth. Clayton sold rabbit pelts, and on one occasion lent some of the proceeds to a friend. This friend lost the money gambling and then told Clayton's brothers that it was Clayton who had lost the money by gambling. While the gambling didn't sit well with his mother, it was Clayton's denial that she reacted to most since she viewed it as the denial of a guilty person. He got the whipping. This made an impression about how much his mother valued honesty. Eventually, the truth came out and, over the years, Clayton reminded his mother that he received a whipping he didn't deserve. She replied that she was sure he had gotten away with some things that did deserve a whipping—one tough lady!

Another story describes one of the ways his mother didn't tolerate disrespect. When Clayton was in Brainerd Junior High School, his teacher was concerned about him and wanted to talk with his mother, so she drove Clayton home from school one day. Clayton pointed to his house, and then proceeded to run away. The teacher called Gladys later that night and expressed her concerns about Clayton getting into trouble and running with the wrong crowd. Gladys lectured Clayton about how he had acted improperly, was disrespectful of his teacher, and that it shouldn't happen again. "She shamed me and I never caused problems for a teacher again. I am appreciative of that lesson."

While Clayton's mother would remind him that he could be whatever he wanted to be, sometimes he needed encouragement and she was there to give it. When Clayton graduated from high school he would have been content to stay in town, work at the Dupont plant, and buy a car. Gladys made sure that he went to college and that he stayed there. After attending his first semester at the University of Tennessee at Knoxville, Clayton was ready to come back home. His mother told him in no uncertain terms that he was to go back to Knoxville, and to not even think about flunking out as a way of escaping. He can't remember whether it was the lecture or the threat of a whipping that kept him in school.

Anyone who has been around Clayton knows how strongly he feels about "giving back." He is very generous himself, and encourages those around him to do what they can. He views it as an obligation that he learned from his mother. As noted earlier, there wasn't a lot of money in the McWhorter household when Clayton was growing up, but there was always something that could be given to the church. Gladys felt this strongly. Even in later years after Clayton had some success in business, she still thought of others. Once Clayton asked her if she needed anything. Her response: "Yes, the parsonage needs painting and we don't have enough money. Could you pay the six hundred dollars?" The giving back of time and money to various community needs began with his mother and has been a big part of Clayton's life ever since.

Gladys had some relatives who were helpful to her in raising the four children. A brother, Wade Dover, and sister-in-law, Selma (wife of her brother Glen), stand out in Clayton's mind as very helpful. Both helped with rides to town, taking the kids to movies, putting a few gifts under the Christmas tree, and more. Wade sometimes supplied some of the discipline the youngsters needed. Clayton recalls, "Uncle Wade wore my butt out once because I put some rocks in my sack of picked cotton to make it heavier. You see, we were paid according to the weight of our picked cotton." So, it appears that Gladys wasn't the only Dover who preached honesty.

The McWhorter siblings, circa 1985: Bernice, Fred, Clayton, and Wayne.

DRAWN INTO PHARMACY

Clayton went off to college at the University of Tennessee, Knoxville, to study pre-pharmacy. After his first year, he transferred to Howard College (now Samford University) in Birmingham, Alabama, to complete his degree and become a licensed pharmacist.

Why did he go down this road? After all, chemistry was not his strong suit and he hated it. There seem to be three parts to the answer. First, his brother Fred was already studying to become a pharmacist. Second, Clayton had worked at L. C. Longley Pharmacy in Rossville, Georgia, while he was in high school. He had gotten to know the pharmacy business and it seemed like a good profession to work in. And third, because of Fred, Clayton had been assured of a part-time job at Vance & Son Pharmacy in Birmingham—this clinched the deal.

The difficult financial circumstances continued throughout his four years in college. Gladys struggled to save money for her children. Clayton was awarded a scholarship from the Walker Drug Company (four hundred dollars) to help him stay in school, and he worked summers and part-time during school at Vance & Son Pharmacy. His work schedule was every afternoon and all day Saturday and Sunday. His starting salary was fifty cents an hour, and during his senior year that was increased to seventy-five cents. Clearly, working those hours and taking a full class schedule impacted his social life. Even Christmas breaks were largely denied because he needed to stay and work.

Clayton's work at both L. C. Longley Pharmacy and Vance & Son Pharmacy did more than just help pay the bills. He learned important lessons about business and about dealing with customers. To know Clayton now, you would never suspect that he once had difficulty interacting with people. He recalls, "I was scared to wait on somebody when they came into the pharmacy. I was embarrassed I wouldn't know what to say." Clearly he has worked through those hang-ups.

One experience burned in him the need to be discreet:

When I was working at L. C. Longley Pharmacy, a man came in and asked, "Where can I find Trojans?" Not knowing what they were, I shouted back to Dr. Longley, "Where can I find the Trojans?" Well this embarrassed the customer, and Dr. Longley sure let me know about that.

Following graduation from pharmacy school, Clayton went to work in the pharmacy owned by his brother Fred in Chattanooga.

PULLED INTO HOSPITAL MANAGEMENT

Despite the love between the two brothers, their working together in the same pharmacy only lasted one year. "I was miserable. Working that close to my brother turned out to be hard on our relationship. For example, I would go out to lunch and when I returned, Fred would ask, 'How was Florida?' He always felt I was gone too long. I also felt confined inside the drugstore."

The economics of both pharmacists working in the same pharmacy didn't work well either. As it turned out, the drugstore couldn't support both their salaries. So Clayton did relief work in other drugstores. While doing this, he met Drew Haskins who told Clayton about a job opening for a pharmacist in Phoebe Putney Memorial Hospital in Albany, Georgia. The assistant administrator of the hospital, Rusty Fetterman, was doing the recruiting, and O. B. Hardy was the administrator. Clayton figured he didn't have anything to lose and applied for the job. With that, Clayton's life turned and an important new chapter began. Clayton recalls:

What I found in the hospital was a pretty scary situation. There really wasn't a pharmacy department, and some community pharmacies were used for most of the prescription work. But nurses were really dispensing the drugs, and there really wasn't anything organizational in place. Nurses would get the drugs, put them in small cups, put them on a tray, and take them to the floors. The community pharmacies were selling a lot of drugs—more than was necessary.

For the first month, I just observed. I was concerned about medication errors, but it took time to purchase equipment, bottles, labels, and everything needed to set up a pharmacy. After that first month, the pharmacy department opened. From that point on, I wasn't very popular with the local pharmacists. But, I had cultivated the support of the hospital's nurses and it worked out well.

After about a year, Rusty Fetterman left the hospital and O. B. Hardy began shifting more responsibilities to Clayton. Besides the pharmacy, he assumed responsibility for a couple of other departments and purchasing. Over time, Clayton hired a pharmacist to replace himself, and he evolved into an assistant administrator.

When Clayton was thirty, O. B. Hardy left the hospital to attend graduate school and later become a consultant. He would eventually reemerge in Clayton's life and play an important role. O. B. recommended Clayton for the job of administrator, but the board thought he was too young. They began recruiting outside candidates. The first candidate who was offered the job told the board he would accept it only if Clayton stayed at the hospital. Clayton didn't think much of him and told him directly, "No sir, you aren't the type of guy I would work for." True to his word, the candidate did not accept the job.

The second candidate was Jesse Reel who had been running a small hospital in Virginia. While Jesse was very polite and made a good appearance on the job, he had difficulty making decisions and relied heavily on Clayton. In this relationship, Clayton learned an important lesson about communication.

Typically, I would go to Jesse and ask him about some situation. "What do you want me to do about it?" Jesse would reply, "Let me think about it." After two or three days, I would repeat the question to Jesse who would respond, "You know what's appropriate, why don't you go ahead and do it?"

After going through this routine several times, I decided it was a waste of time. So I quit taking situations to Jesse and just handled them myself. Well, one day Jesse came to me all upset. "I am administrator of the hospital and not consulted anymore." I responded, "Yes sir, but I go into your office and you just procrastinate. Then in two or three days you tell me to go ahead and handle the situation. It's a waste of time." Jesse was taken aback, but stated, "I deserve to know what's going on, even if you make the decisions. You come and tell me." I sure got the point, saying, "Yes sir, you are right about that. I should have done it."

With O. B. Hardy and Rusty Fetterman gone, Clayton concluded that he needed a change. A friend of his, Terry Hiers, was leaving the administrator's position of Sumter County Hospital in Americus, Georgia. Terry suggested that Clayton apply. With a recommendation from O. B. Hardy and Gene Kidd (then administrator of Baptist Hospital in Nashville, but formerly administrator of a hospital in Albany, Georgia), Clayton applied to the three-person search committee that former president Jimmy Carter chaired.

Before he could leave Albany, Clayton was confronted by a board member who prided himself in how many "asses he had whipped." Clayton had gotten crossways with him before because he didn't take his attitude. And his applying for another job made the situation even worse. This board member told Clayton, "I can't believe you're pulling up stakes and leaving here." Clayton responded, "Well, it's people like you who would want to make people leave." The board member responded, "Let me tell you young man, I know a lot of people in Americus, Georgia. All I have to do is make one phone call and tell them about you and you wouldn't be able to go there." Clayton bluffed, "I already talked to people up there and told them what kind of a person you are. The best recommendation for me would be for you to call and tell them that I am a jerk." Apparently the board member never made the call; Clayton got the job and moved to Americus, Georgia.

During Clayton's tenure as administrator of Sumter County Hospital, his managerial and leadership skills were further developed and his experience base broadened by the challenges he faced. As a county hospital in a poor county, the financial situation was always tight. Accounts payable and accounts receivable were managed daily, with a priority system that always left some older than they should have been and many past due . . . there just wasn't the cash.

One situation Clayton recalls really helped test his mettle. He was there at a time when the federal government had passed both the Civil Rights law (1964) and the Medicare law (1965).

I had to integrate the hospital. Sumter County Hospital was literally two separate hospitals with two entrances, two nurseries, and two business offices, with the only common thing being the operating room. It was my job to lead the hospital through integration. Federal inspectors were coming down to inspect the hospital in order to qualify it for Medicare. I had already received death threats and was scared. The Georgia Bureau of Investigation was notified, but I still felt threatened. Fortunately, I had developed good relationships with the medical and hospital staff. It was an explosive situation with marches and Dr. Martin Luther King having already been jailed in Americus.

In speaking with the physicians, I was told there was no way we could admit black patients on the "white" side, unless it was in a private room (of which we had very few). We came up with a solution. We lined up ten white "patients" (community members who volunteered to help) and admitted them to the "colored" side, and sharing rooms in a few cases with black patients. We set up charts for these patients, and when the inspectors came through, the hospital passed. This was a necessary ruse because it bought time to do the integration properly.

Ironically, the NAACP publically charged the hospital with "forcing colored employees to be patients in order to pass the inspection." This made the national news, so here came the Feds again. They wanted the charts of all the black patients in the hospital on the day of the earlier inspection. We gave them the charts, which they reviewed. Going further, they confirmed through interviews that those patients had indeed had major surgeries, babies, etc., all legitimate reasons for being in the hospital. The Feds concluded, "There was no basis for the allegation," and left. They had not thought to investigate the charts of the white patients.

In retrospect, I did the right thing. The only board member who really challenged me was Jimmy Carter, claiming it was dishonest. But we had a crisis to deal with, my life was being threatened; yet we had the continued obligation of treating patients, we had to keep the hospital afloat. No, it wasn't totally honest, but it was a strategic move that helped us work through an explosive situation.

From Americus, Clayton was recruited to be the administrator of City-County Hospital in LaGrange, Georgia. The board at Sumter County Hospital tried to retain Clayton by offering to match his new salary of twenty-five thousand dollars. Clayton's position was that the board felt they were paying him appropriately at seventeen thousand dollars, and somebody had offered a bigger hospital with more money which he had already accepted, so he was leaving.

The hospital in LaGrange was strongly supported by the Callaway family. They owned the Callaway Mills that were later sold to Milliken Industries. Perrin Collier, a former executive of Callaway Mills, was the chairman of the board at the hospital and he took Clayton under his wing.

It was a good thing he had that support, because the first major challenge he faced was with the medical staff. From the previous administration, Clayton inherited an adversarial relationship between administration and the medical staff. For the first time in his career, he was informed that he could not attend medical staff meetings. His reaction was, *Well, this administration is going to attend.*

One of my assistant administrators warned me that the medical staff would kick me out of the meeting if I tried to attend. So, acting like I didn't know any better, I went to the first medical staff meeting. Prior to the meeting, I'd gotten a little friendly with Dr. Holder who was chief of staff. So at the meeting, before somebody asked me to leave, I asked Dr. Holder if I could make a statement as the new administrator since there were a number of physicians in attendance that I had not personally met by that time. So I introduced myself as the new hospital administrator, and I went on to say that I understood that there was a policy in the past that administrators were not welcome at the medical staff meeting. I said, "Gentlemen, we're all in this game together. You can check me out A through Z, I am pro-physician. You are my customer. Without you, we don't need this place, we don't need the beds, because without you, we wouldn't have any patients. I can understand your concerns and issues, and I will not go out and broadcast anything that is confidential. But for me to be an effective hospital administrator, to be your sponsor to nurses and department heads and everybody else, and so we can make this the best hospital we all want, I need to understand you and be involved with you. And that is my message." The chief of staff said, "Mr. McWhorter, please have a seat, you are welcome." And from that point on, I went to medical staff meetings. I worked hard at medical staff relationships. I believed any administrator that didn't was stupid.

Working smart with the medical staff didn't always mean rolling over for everyone. On the staff of City-County Hospital was Dr. Hilt Hammett, an ENT who was big like a bulldog. He was tough and loved to chew up people and then spit them out. He was one of those who would throw a golf club at a tree if he screwed up a shot. Clayton recalls:

One day he came into my office and set a tray of food on my table and said, "You eat it." I replied, "I'm not hungry, Doctor." He then proceeded to chew out my rear end about the bad food in the hospital. While he was shouting and screaming, I walked around my desk and quietly opened my office door and closed it behind me. When he realized I wasn't there, he opened the door and asked, "Where are you going?" I went back in the office and said, "Doctor, when you can come in to my office and talk to me like a decent human being, I'll listen to you. I'm not hard of hearing, and you don't scream at me. Do you understand?" Do you know what his answer was?

Back then I had some plaques on the wall and certificates from my pharmacy school and he said, "Damn it, I forgot, you understand the medical profession because of your background." From that point on, he pretty much left me alone.

During Clayton's last year and a half at the hospital, a major hospital modernization program was being planned. Approximately two-thirds of the hospital had been built in the 1930s or earlier and had become inadequate. Working with Hill Burton program administrators in Atlanta, the Callaway Foundation, and local officials, funding of the project was going to be a third Hill Burton money, a third from the Callaway Foundation and the remaining third a city bond issue requiring approval by voters. Unfortunately, the first vote to approve the bond issue failed by approximately one hundred votes.

During this modernization and expansion campaign, Clayton had been approached by HCA. Bob Brueck had brought Clayton to Nashville to discuss opening a hospital in Albany, Georgia. Paul McKnight, HCA's human resources director, picked Clayton up at the airport and brought him to the corporate headquarters for the recruiting pitch. Clayton's response was, "We're involved in an important campaign. I've got this modernization and expansion program that I'm obligated to complete, and I just can't go to Albany." As luck would have it, word of the bond issue's failure reached Dr. Charles Gillespie, an orthopedic surgeon in Albany. He called Dr. Thomas "Tommy" Frist Jr., informing him that the time might be right for HCA to approach Clayton again. Clayton recalls:

It was a Saturday, and I was at the LaGrange Country Club getting ready to hit off the first tee. The Pro Shop notified me that I had an urgent call in their office. I took the call and it was Tommy Frist, asking if I would consider going to Albany. I told Tommy that I would need to think about it. He said, "Clayton, the doctors really want you down there. They think you're the person who can go in and make that successful. I'll pay you what I'm making. I'm making $30,000 a year, so will you take the job for $30,000?"

There was a car and other things that went along with the job. I said it sounded good because it was more money than I was making in my current situation. He said that he needed a decision soon. I struggled with the decision, but finally decided to go.

Perrin Collier, the board chairman of City-County Hospital, was upset and asked how Clayton could leave them and told him how important it was for him to stay and resurrect the bond issue. He asked what Clayton was getting that they couldn't provide. Clayton responded, "Right now, the better challenge." He could see something beyond a one-hospital deal, and he took the risky step of moving into the fledgling investor-owned hospital management sector. HCA was just two years old with fewer than twenty hospitals.

THOMAS FRIST JR.
Founder and later CEO, chairman, and
chairman of the executive committee of HCA

When we were building Palmyra Park Hospital in Albany, GA, we wanted the very best CEO . . . someone that was people friendly, had good humanistic skills, and a track record of great relationships with physicians. There was already a major competitor in Albany and we had some of the leading physicians as board members. We turned to them for advice. We needed someone that could almost walk on water since building this hospital was a big bet for what was still a young, entrepreneurial company. Well I got a call from Dr. Charles Gillespie, an orthopedic surgeon in Albany. He told me there was an extremely bright, young and up-and-coming administrator at the hospital in LaGrange. He gave me his number and said we might be able to attract him to take on the challenge and join this company. Through a series of calls he made a career-defining decision, showing one of his skills . . . he is a risk taker.

CLIMBING THE HCA LADDER

HCA has been an operations-driven company where successful hospital management was almost a prerequisite for advancement in the ranks. So it was fitting that Clayton's start at HCA was in running a hospital.

As Clayton was overseeing the construction of Palmyra Park Hospital in Albany, Georgia, identical facilities were being constructed in Macon, Georgia, and Chattanooga, Tennessee. The corporate office proved to be "a little thin" in support for the three administrators: Clayton in Albany, John Conroy in Chattanooga, and Jack Frayer in Macon. These three became a support team for each other. For example, each one needed operation and procedure manuals for each of their hospital departments. Clayton, John, and Jack split up the departments and shared their work with each other so that each had a complete and identical package. The three hospitals were opened on consecutive weekends and each of the administrators attended the dedication of the other two's hospital opening.

Clayton recalls the early days with his hospital. Challenges began the day of dedication when a painter spilled paint on a new hallway carpet. An hour before the official dedication, the carpet was replaced and the doors were opened on schedule. Batey Gresham, the architect, and Clayton went around to local furniture stores buying wall hangings and other decorations. The operating rooms couldn't be used for the first two weeks because of a conductivity problem. Doctors were a little reluctant to put medical patients into the hospital that wasn't performing surgery. Clayton began to wonder what he had gotten himself into.

Problems continued as a number of physicians who had promised to support the hospital if Clayton came back to Albany didn't admit patients in the very beginning. Clayton had to get on the phone and raise hell with them, threatening to leave. He describes his actions as, "Marketing the hell out of them." He believes he spent approximately 50 percent of the first year doing nothing but physician recruiting, calling on them in their offices, and making the case for why it was important for the HCA hospital to be successful. He spent an hour and a half at the beginning of each day in the doctor's lounge. True to his reputation, he won over enough of the medical community for the hospital to be successful.

When HCA opened up Palmyra Park, it became a competing hospital to Phoebe Putney Memorial Hospital where Clayton had previously been an assistant administrator. Jesse Reel was still administrator of Phoebe Putney and made it very clear to Clayton that there would be absolutely no cooperation between the two hospitals. Clayton recalls:

> Well, what he didn't know was that I already knew everything I wanted to know about his hospital. Because of prior relationships, I had his whole payroll . . . what everybody made. I didn't solicit this information, but people volunteered it to me. Jesse had apparently forgotten that I had been there all those years and had developed some strong relationships. I staffed Palmyra Park Hospital with the people that I knew; my frontline talent came and no one that I offered a job to turned me down. I was able to offer employees slightly higher salaries knowing what they were currently making.

Operating within the HCA structure presented new lessons and opportunities. Before the hospital opened, Clayton had submitted a budget to the corporate office. Soon after, an accountant from the corporate office called to say that they didn't like his budget. Clayton asked what he didn't like, and he said, "The bottom line needs to be bigger." Clayton then asked what he wanted it to be. He was given a figure, and then said, "Good. I'll have it to you tomorrow." Clayton then submitted the budget that the accountant wanted, and included a note saying, "Here's your budget, but this [some different number] is what I think we're going to make."

HCA's hospital operations were divided into regional divisions. Clayton reported to a division vice president (DVP) in Atlanta, named Bob Crosby. Bob's financial person was Jim Main. Bob, Jim, and Clayton all became good friends. The company employed a concept called "regional administrators." Basically, a regional administrator had two or three hospitals that they worked with in addition to running their own hospital. It was another way of using good talent when somebody encountered a problem so the DVP wouldn't have to spread himself so thin. Clayton was tapped to be a regional administrator, and recalls some really challenging situations. One example was a hospital in Miami where, "The doctors were just awful to deal with. You put out a fire and the next day you'd have another big one."

After about three years as the administrator in Albany, the division vice president position in Atlanta became available. Clayton was selected for that position, and a new chapter began. The multi-facility manager role at HCA was very demanding and required different skills than running a hospital. Hospital administrators were independent people in the HCA decentralized management structure. The multi-facility manager had to coach, cajole, reason with, and in some cases threaten, the administrator; but the administrator still made many of the decisions. Jim Main remained as assistant vice president of finance. Clayton's hospitals in this old "Division 3" were located in Florida, Georgia, the Carolinas, and Virginia. Clayton recalls:

> We had a great team, we had good administrators, we had a good structure, and we worked hard and played hard. We had meetings and, I hate to admit it, sometimes we stayed up most of the night and still got up the next morning to function. We just developed a wonderful relationship within the division and within HCA.

Clayton's team of administrators in Division 3 included several people who went on to hold executive-level positions within HCA's corporate structure. This included: Dave Williamson who headed up the company's development function until his death in the mid-eighties, Jack Bovender who is currently HCA's chief executive officer (CEO), and Sam Owen who later replaced Clayton as DVP and also ran the HCA physician services company in the early eighties.

Clayton remained in this DVP role from 1973 until 1977, when he was given an opportunity to move to Nashville. The circumstances around the promotion to senior vice president of operations began a year earlier. In the fall of 1976, the then chairman and CEO, John Hill, called Clayton to Nashville. Clayton was quickly put in an uncomfortable position when he was asked his opinion about who should replace John Neff, the current president and chief operating officer (COO). Apparently, John Neff had done some things that prompted Jack Massey, Dr. Thomas Frist Sr., and Tommy Frist Jr. to call for his removal. Clayton was asked whether John Neff's replacement should be Tommy Frist Jr. or Bob Brueck. Clayton responded, "I think Bob Brueck should be the guy . . . he's the one who understands the business." John Hill indicated there was a big push from the Frist family for Tommy Frist Jr. Clayton responded, "Tommy just hasn't been there. He is great at acquisitions, development, and finding spots to build hospitals. But if the position needs an operational guy, then it's Bob Brueck. He has really done a good job running the hospitals and developing the company's policies and procedures."

The decision was deferred for several months and Jack Massey moved into the president's position. During that period, a consultant was hired to evaluate various people for executive positions. In the fall of 1977, decisions were made. Tommy Frist Jr. would become president and COO. Jack Massey offered the position of executive vice president for operations to Clayton. He was surprised because he thought Bob Brueck was running operations. Jack Massey responded, "It's time for a change. Mr. Brueck will be doing something else, but it is not going to be running operations." Clayton didn't immediately accept because he didn't want to move from Atlanta. Well this changed with a phone call from Tommy Frist. He informed Clayton, "If you don't accept this, you know who the back-up is." Clayton recalls, "I never truly believed that this was the case, but they knew that I wouldn't work for their back-up person, so I said, 'I'll take it.'"

The promotion required relocation to Nashville. Clayton's wife of thirteen years, Angelyn (Angel), informed him that she wasn't going to leave Atlanta. Their divorce was final shortly after that, and Clayton moved to Nashville. One awkward aspect of this situation related to Clayton's relationship with Bob Brueck. Bob had been his friend and mentor. Yet in the end, when Bob was pushed aside, Clayton replaced

Clayton McWhorter, Dr. Thomas Frist Jr., and Dave Williamson at HCA's Data Center, 1984.

him. Bob went on to establish the Center for Health Studies, which was the planning, research, and education arm of HCA for ten years. It had been a concept of Bob's for several years previously, and Clayton became one of its biggest supporters. During the years that Clayton ran operations, he sought advice and counsel from Bob Brueck more than anyone else, even after Bob retired in 1983.

The executive team that was put together after this shake-up remained intact during HCA's rapid growth spurt in the late seventies and early eighties. Clayton was executive vice president for operations, Dave Williamson was executive vice president of development, Sam Brooks was chief financial officer (CFO), and Bob Crosby returned to HCA and ran the international division. This group worked together and became good friends.

The working relationship between Clayton and Dave Williamson reflected a business philosophy of: "you acquire them, we'll run them." Clayton felt that people in hospital operations would be terrible at acquisitions. They would go in to size up an operation and only see the operating difficulties. He was thankful that Dave Williamson ran acquisitions; otherwise he thinks HCA's growth would have been severely stunted.

That's not to say that operations didn't have their issues with the acquisitions group. Members of Dave's acquisition staff often made promises that were then handed over to operations to fulfill. Clayton instituted a "promise audit" to try and rein in the practice.

Between 1977 and 1987, Clayton's role evolved. At one point, Bob Crosby left HCA and Clayton assumed responsibility for international

An HCA management meeting, circa 1974. From left to right: Joe DiLorenzo, John Colton, Jim Main, Andrew (Woody) Miller, Clayton McWhorter, Roger Mick, Bud Adams, Chuck Ederer, and John Tobin.

operations. In 1981, HCA acquired Hospital Affiliates International and General Care Corporation. Clayton's operations group had the major task of absorbing a large group of owned and managed hospitals.

In the early 1980s, hospital companies including HCA went through a variety of experiments with non-hospital health-care diversifications. HCA experimented with health insurance, physician services companies, home health-care companies, clinical research, venture capital, psychiatric hospitals, etc. Most of these initiatives did not work out for HCA. However, the Nashville health-care community benefited as these companies were spun off. Also, the laid-off executives tended to stay in Nashville to start up similar companies.

Perhaps the biggest initiative was the attempted merger with American Hospital Supply Company, the largest in the business. An agreement had been reached and the new company was going to be named Kuron. Carl Bays, chairman and CEO of American Hospital Supply, and Tommy Frist had already begun working out the organizational chart of the merged companies. Carl Bays and a couple of his executives attended

And there were sports . . . HCA management was challanged by the HCA Women's Basketball Team, circa 1982. The picture shows "HTI Globetrotting" Bob Crosby, Dr. Thomas Frist Sr., "Mitey-Mite" Roger Mick, and "Macho-Macho Man" Clayton McWhorter.

what was to be HCA's last formal board meeting before the merger. Shortly after the meeting everything began to unravel. First, there was a lot of noise from American Hospital Supply Company's customers in the nonprofit hospital sector. They viewed HCA as a major competitive threat and didn't see the logic in buying products from a competitor. Then Vernon Loucks, CEO of Baxter Travenol, a smaller supply company, approached Tommy indicating his interest in buying the larger American Hospital Supply. When the dust settled, Baxter Travenol did acquire American Hospital Supply and paid HCA $150 million for breaking up the deal.

In the end, the variety of diversification efforts failed to offset the revenue and earnings pressures created by the diagnostic-related group (DRG) reimbursement system, the increased competition for in-patient and out-patient services among hospitals, and state regulatory programs restricting expansion and, in some cases, pricing. HCA's earnings suffered and the stock price plummeted. While this was occurring, Donald S. MacNaughton vacated the chairman of the board position and remained chairman of the executive committee of the board, Tommy Frist became chairman and CEO, and Clayton become a member of the HCA board as well as president and COO.

Chapter Two

THE HEALTHTRUST STORY

WHY HEALTHTRUST?

HealthTrust, Inc. (HTI) began as a solution to one of HCA's problems. In 1986 HCA disappointed Wall Street. After eighteen consecutive years of earning per share growth, 1986 earnings before extraordinary items declined 38 percent. HCA's exemplary earnings record of 30 percent compound annual growth from 1976 through 1985 abruptly became history and Wall Street was not kind. The stock price fell and there was tremendous pressure for the company to recover its historic growth rate. While some of the problem lay with the shift in Medicare's hospital reimbursement to a prospective payment methodology and a concurrent drop in hospital utilization rates, some of the problem was attributed to corporate overhead costs and an accumulated group of underperforming hospitals that diluted the consolidated earnings growth of the company.

The blow to the stock price was itself a penalty, but there was an even greater threat associated with the ability of corporate raiders who were very active at that time to take over even large companies using junk (high yield) bond financing. They were looking for and acquiring undervalued companies. The result of these unfriendly takeovers included breaking up companies into parts that were then sold to the highest bidders, drastic reductions in operating cost, etc. If HCA were acquired in this fashion, the whole culture of the company would likely have been destroyed.

HCA proceeded with a two-pronged strategy that included cutting its operating costs and pruning its portfolio of hospitals and related businesses. Clayton describes the budget reviews as involving give-and-take between Tommy Frist Jr. and himself. Each had their "sacred cows" and targets. In the year leading up to HTI's creation, corporate costs were reduced and functions downsized.

More relevant to HTI's creation were the efforts to identify a group of hospitals that could be sold to other owners or spun off into an independent company. The original list included approximately 120 hospitals that were underperforming and did not have good prospects going foward. It was realized that there weren't any viable buyers in the market for such a large group of hospitals. The operative assumption was that a buyer would have to be created.

HCA would not take an earnings hit, and the spin-off company would need to have a chance of success given the debt service requirements associated with a fair purchase price. Options ranged from putting the hospitals into a "not-for-profit" corporation with a long-term management contract back to HCA, to an offer from Charlie Martin (senior vice president (SVP) of development at HCA) to take the "dog hospitals" and show what he could do. HCA recognized that

Charlie Martin, Governor Ned Ray McWherter, and Clayton McWhorter during HealthTrust's first management conference in 1987.

Federal Legislation sponsored by Senator Russell Long, (D. LA) created the ESOP structure that allowed HCA's spin-off of HealthTrust to occur. At HealthTrust's first management conference in 1987 Senator Long (left) visits with Donald MacNaughton.

pruning its portfolio of hospitals with proper financial consideration would improve the performance of the consolidated group of remaining hospitals. What was missing for some time was a financially viable way of spinning off the hospitals.

The Gestation Period

The missing link on how to structure the transaction was found during a meeting on Sunday, March 1, 1987. For several months preceding that meeting, Clayton and other members of the senior management team had been working with a consultant, Ram Charan, on strategy, restructuring, and execution matters. Toward the end of this particular meeting, and after a few of the participants had left, Clayton casually asked Ram if he had any suggestions on how to structure the spin-off of a large group of hospitals, explaining that efforts so far had not identified a viable approach. Ram quickly suggested that HCA look at an Employee Stock Ownership Plan (ESOP). Ram had just joined the board of a company in Pittsburgh that was structured as an ESOP. Ironically, a presentation by Bankers Trust the preceding summer had included the ESOP in a laundry list of possible approaches. The idea was not pursued until after Ram's suggestion. It was explored quickly and judged to be viable—HTI was conceived.

By the time of HTI's birth on September 17, 1987, several things had occurred that shaped the "what's and how's" of its seven-and-a-half year life. First, the list of the 120 hospitals slated for spin off was trimmed to 104. Most of the 16 hospitals dropped from the list were going to require significant capital infusions in the succeeding three years . . . something HTI would not be able to afford. Additionally, a few hospitals were removed from the list because of commitments that HCA felt uncomfortable breaking. The 104 hospitals that became HTI's initial operating base were a mixture of hospitals with a wide range of opportunities. Many were quickly seen as good growth opportunities; however, there were some that had no real future as part of HCA or HTI. Clayton says, "If I had known I was going into HTI at the time the hospitals were identified, I wouldn't have picked some of the hospitals we picked."

THOMAS FRIST JR.

There was somewhat of a wrestling match because you're taking two strong personalities in Clayton and Charlie [Martin] and putting them over there together. Both had different styles, different motivations, and what drives them. But I felt they had something that in a highly leveraged situation would allow them to execute and hit the homerun. While they both brought attributes to the table, I wasn't completely confident that if I put them over there by themselves that they would get the results. So I asked Don MacNaughton, who I admired a lot, who had been a mentor of mine to go with them. He needed to make sure that Clayton and Charlie got along—act as a referee and a wise sage— especially during the first year.

Another set of decisions involved selecting the group of executives that would set up and run HTI. The nucleus of the management team were the "3-M's": Clayton McWhorter (HCA's president and COO), Don MacNaughton (HCA's chairman of the executive committee of the board), and Charlie Martin (HCA's senior vice president of development). These men were invited to lead HTI as a group, and provide credibility to the investment community for the large amount of debt that would have to be incurred in the purchase of 104 hospitals. The three selected the next level of executives that would be their direct reports from the cadre of managers at HCA. The original officer group and their HTI titles were:

- Don MacNaughton, chairman of the Executive Committee of the Board
- Clayton McWhorter, CEO and chairman of the board
- Charlie Martin, president and COO
- Hilary (Bud) Adams, vice president of development
- Mike Koban, vice president of finance
- Ken Donahey, vice president and controller
- Richard Gaston, vice president of administration
- John Hyde, vice president of support services
- David Smith, vice president of internal audit
- Bob Vraciu, vice president of strategic planning and marketing services
- Steve Brandt, regional vice president of operations
- Leon Hooper, regional vice president of operations
- Jim Dalton, regional vice president of operations
- Stuart Voelpel, regional vice president of operations
- Jim Main, regional vice president of operations

(The appendix lists the corporate employees that made the journey to HTI in 1987.)

Clayton viewed this team as a diverse group of capable executives who weren't shy about expressing their views. Most had been the number one or number two person in their respective corporate functions at HCA and the regional vice presidents of operations had held similar positions at HCA. HCA had only declared a handful of people "off-limits." This didn't present any problems to Clayton, who still believes that he got the best team for the hospitals HTI acquired and considering the pressures that HTI faced.

THOMAS FRIST JR.

I have always been a proponent of spinning out businesses when it was appropriate; and it certainly was appropriate at this time [1987] to take a group of hospitals with some common characteristics and so much stress on the industry. With the right leadership I thought this group of hospitals [HealthTrust] could do well. Clayton certainly played a key role in the architecture of the spin-off. What he didn't know was my plan to basically take the top management group from HCA and put them with HealthTrust, then promote their protégés into the top positions at HCA. It was like shock therapy for both organizations. It provided for new blood, new ways of looking at things and new enthusiasm, and not being in a rut. Clayton and I and others had been together and through so many battles over the years. The management that went to HealthTrust still had so much energy; they just needed a new challenge. And the management remaining at HCA needed rejuvenating after going through such tough times. But I remember vividly that during the few months from when the management team for HealthTrust was decided and when the spin-off occurred there we so many emotions—from first, the feeling of rejection, then "Why me?", then, "Can it be successful with so much debt?" We ended up putting a lot of guarantees into it, so I felt reassured that not only would they do well, they would do extremely well.

This group had a relatively unique opportunity in May 1987. They were able to construct the corporate structure and define the functions and philosophy of a new company that would begin with $1.6 billion of annual revenue. During an early planning meeting, the group defined the heart of HTI's operating model. Notes from the May 27–28, 1987, Organizational Planning Meeting accurately captured the operating philosophy employed by HTI:

Decentralized Management Philosophy: Hospital administrators are in the best position to make decisions and understand circumstances; ensure best administrator in position; risk taking desired—mistakes tolerated; emphasis on results, not how something is done.

Small Corporate Staff: High percentage of variable costs; quick decision making; few managers—mostly doers; error on side of too few rather

HealthTrust's regional vice presidents of operations, 1987: Jim Main, Jim Dalton, Leon Hooper, Stuart Voelpel, and Steve Brandt.

than too many employees; effective communications; few amenities; emphasize self-implementation (i.e., no implementation staff at corporate); fewer meetings and committees.

Teamwork Approach: Avoid "we—they" attitude; cross training of staff so they can carry out multiple functions.

Employees will have a clear understanding of what is expected of them and be held accountable for results: Clear communication; avoid mercenary look; aggressively set targets; establish "6" specific primary objectives.

Compensation Closely Related to Performance: Seventy-five to 100 percent of base maximum bonuses for administrators; compensate based on contribution—not the number of employees.

Quality and Service Philosophy: Develop reputation with physicians and patients for service; monitor perception; different communities have different levels of need/expectations; can add back $6/hr nurse aides instead of $15/hr RNs and have more hands-on service in appropriate circumstances.

Physician Orientation: Still key to success; be more aggressive/ flexible; increase number of active admitters 50 percent; treat medical communities individually.

Aggressively Pursue Revenue Building Opportunities: Physicians— recruit and market to; new services and products; alternate uses of excess capacity; each market is different; corporate may impose solutions.

Standardization of Select Systems: Administrator still in best position to make decisions and understand circumstances; emphasis on results, not how something is done; some standardization decisions made by corporate, presumably with agreement by Regional VPs of Operations; line management has responsibility for results.

Asset Management and Debt Repayment: Tightly manage capital expenditures, A/R, A/P, staffing and benefits; quickly divest 20 hospitals; daily, weekly, and monthly reports; repay debt quickly.

Of course, these philosophical points needed to be operationalized and a detailed plan developed. Individuals brought their plans into group meetings that had a peculiar set of moods. Everyone knew how serious the situation was because there would be no margin for error; but there was almost giddiness to some discussions. Everyone was off on a new adventure where both the risks and the rewards were high.

The other critical set of decisions revolved around the deal structure that defined HTI's capital structure and HCA's payment for the 104 hospitals. As mentioned above, the ESOP solution made the transaction viable. The primary reason was that holders of the ESOP debt were entitled to exclude from taxable income 50 percent of the interest received. This, of course, lowered the cost of capital to HTI. The initial capital structure was:

ESOP Bank Debt	$540mm
Bank Debt	$400mm
ESOP Senior Notes	$270mm
Senior Subordinate Notes	$286mm
Subordinated Debentures	$240mm
TOTAL LONG TERM DEBT	$1,736mm
Preferred Stock A&B	$460mm
Common Stock	$4mm
TOTAL EQUITY	$464mm
TOTAL CAPITALIZATION	$2,200mm

There was no mistake! This was a highly leveraged purchase of HCA's underperforming hospitals. Drexel Burnham Lambert, an investment-banking firm, was the lead in raising the $1.736 billion in debt. Michael Milken, the head of their high yield (alias junk bond) division, couldn't get the deal done without HCA's guarantee of some of the debt. For this guarantee and further consideration of the sale of the hospitals, HCA received the $464mm in preferred stock (with escalating dividend payments) and warrants to purchase 35 percent of HTI's common stock. After a long "road show," and a few investors' doors opened by Don MacNaughton, the deal was completed on September 17, 1987.

HCA made a few additional requirements of HTI. It held a position on the HTI board, filled by Vic Campbell, and HTI was required to purchase HCA's package of information systems, remain in their group purchasing program and government affairs program, use the same labor attorneys, and compensation decisions for McWhorter and Martin had to be approved by HCA.

*Left: Dapper Bud Adams, on the tailgate of a moving truck, personally supervised the move from HCA offices to HealthTrust's offices in 1987. **Right:** Donald MacNaughton and Dr. Thomas Frist Sr., 1987.*

Clearly HTI faced significant management challenges as a result of the large amount of debt, the escalating dividend payments, etc. There was some good fortune in the timing of the transaction. On October 19, 1987, barely one month after the transaction, the market crashed 24 percent in one day. Following the crash, a deal like HTI's could not have been completed.

During the spring and early summer of 1987, the spin-off was called Newco (a conventional investment bankers' term for a company in the planning stages). Management kicked around a lot of different names, including funny ones like "Hospitals R Us." Clayton came up with the name HealthTrust following a SunTrust Bank board meeting where he saw "SunTrust" prominently displayed on each slide shown on the screen. Well, HealthTrust was an easy derivative of SunTrust and he knew quickly that "it had to be the name of the company." There were some legal problems using "Trust" (with a capital T) in the name of a non-banking company in Texas; however the lawyers got creative, and HealthTrust replaced Newco as the name of HCA's spin-off company.

In the summer of 1987, a group of 130 people packed their belongings in their HCA offices and moved about five miles away to 4525 Harding Road, into a building whose long-term lease was acquired six years earlier with the purchase of Hospital Affiliates. This move brought a mixture of emotions to the new HTI employees. There was anxiety associated with the risky venture; and there was excitement associated with a new adventure and the opportunities it brought. Clayton felt like he was "moving from the mother house to the condo." He had been with HCA since 1970; much of the HTI team had been there for many years as well. As for Clayton's reaction to media reports that HTI had taken HCA's "dogs" he was fond of saying, "We will turn those dogs into greyhounds."

HTI's first month of operation was both busy and lonely. First, management was faced with the reality of "the deal." Most of the terms were a cram-down by HCA. The valuations attached to the hospitals and the financial structure of HTI were largely stacked in HCA's favor. The way in which these terms had been dictated to HTI strained the relationships between people who had worked shoulder-to-shoulder for many years within HCA. Two things were apparent. The warrants held by HCA to purchase 35 percent of HTI's stock essentially gave HCA first claim on any value HTI was able to create in the first few years. This was a high price to pay for the loan guarantees that HCA had given on some of the debt and for assuming liability for the hospitals' actions prior to HTI's acquisition. Also, HTI had to position itself to restructure its capital in just a few years. The preferred stock issued to HCA had dividends payable "in kind" until October 1, 1992; thereafter, a significant cash dividend payment would be required each quarter. This was viewed as a financial time bomb since it would strip HTI of cash necessary for investing in its hospitals.

The second part of the reality shock actually began the summer before the deal was completed. In most cases, the hospitals that made up HTI's group of 104 had little visibility with the corporate offices. Thus, management had a steep learning curve as it tried to understand the hospitals, their markets, and what it would take to improve their performance. Any remorse management had about leaving HCA was quickly replaced with the busyness associated with an aggressive management agenda and a great sense of urgency.

MAKING IT WORK

By the time the deal was completed on September 17, 1987, HTI managers in field operations were already sprinting. Reporting relationships of the hospitals had shifted from HCA to HTI on June 22, 1987, and operations were already three months into their assessments and early interventions.

From June 29 through July 23, each hospital CEO had a one-hour strategy review of their hospital's situation with a six-person team from the corporate office that included: Charlie Martin, Bob Vraciu, Bud Adams, Ken Donahey, John Hyde, and that particular hospital's operation vice president. On the surface, the strategy review was intended to give the corporate team an overview of the hospital's situation, its potential in its market, resource requirements, especially capital, and to become familiar with the hospital CEO. From the hospital CEO's side of the table, he or she viewed the meeting as an anxious job interview.

Hospital CEOs were asked to make a presentation that covered: (a) an analysis of their hospital's marketplace and the hospital's position within it; (b) the five or six things that the hospital could do in the next year to improve its performance; (c) resource requirements such as capital, support services, etc.; and (d) a little bit about themselves.

The meetings proved to be highly interactive and informative. As a result, some things were realized. Approximately twenty of the hospitals showed little potential under HTI's ownership. The root causes ranged from a medical staff that could not be improved to hospitals being located in highly competitive markets with little competitive advantage. Also, capital requirements in the short term were not going to be excessive. HCA had not capital-starved these hospitals, and they were in pretty good shape.

Patterns about hospital situations and strategies began to emerge, typically around their market situation. Three prototypes described most of HTI's hospitals: those that were the only hospital in their community; those in a two-hospital community; and those in an urban market where the HTI hospital was a small player. These groupings tended to guide the types of general hospital strategies that were pursued. Peer groups of hospitals were formed to share experiences and best practices with other hospitals within each group. Since they had similiar circumstances, they found similiar challenges and similiar solutions.

Hospital CEOs got fast approvals and encouragement for reasonable initiatives that would quickly impact their hospital's performance. Twenty-three hospital CEOs were judged to be underperforming in their current situations. Hospital performance was expected to improve with a change in CEO. Seven hospitals had CEOs who were in the process of being transferred or retiring, and three hospitals had CEOs who were doing a good job, but had indicated their desire to move to a different hospital. As it worked out, after eighteen months, sixty hospital CEO changes had occurred.

The exceptional operating talent of Charlie Martin, COO, showed itself quickly. He was quick to assess situations and zero in on the real issues. He was quick to decide what would or would not be done, thus giving hospital CEOs timely decisions. Charlie's aptitude for analysis put the heat on everyone to be prepared in their meetings lest they "get blown out of the water."

During those early months, the company set two short-term imperatives: improve cash flow and pay down its debt. These imperatives were attacked with a five-prong approach:

1. Ensuring competent and motivated managers in each hospital
   • Change out hospital CEOs who are underperforming.
   • Provide necessary direction and incentives for all CEOs.
   • Implement an administrator bonus program that rewards, among other things, cash-flow improvement.

2. Price increases where and when appropriate

3. Improve and motivate hospital medical staffs
   • Pursue joint-venture opportunities already on the table.
   • Recruit physicians aggressively.
   • Have Clayton McWhorter, Charlie Martin, and the regional vice presidents visit hospitals quickly and reassure the medical staff of HealthTrust's commitments, and seek their help in growing the hospital's business.
   • Provide hospital CEO incentives for recruiting physicians from competing hospitals.

4. Improve hospital efficiency by 5 percent within six months

HealthTrust's executive management team, 1987: Donald MacNaughton, Clayton McWhorter, and Charlie Martin.

- Implement standardized approaches to Dietary, Housekeeping, Business Office, Medical Records, and Maintenance.
- Implement productivity standards companywide.

5. Asset management
   - Quickly divest hospitals that do not have the potential for improvement.
   - Improve materials management and inventory management.
   - Sell excess land around hospitals.
   - Sell physician office buildings to outside groups, typically, real estate investment trusts.

Clayton believed from the beginning that HTI should act as though it were a public company even though it was private. He disclosed quarterly results and met frequently with analysts who followed the hospital management companies. He ensured that HTI had a history of improving earnings so that when the time came for an "exit," there would be a good track record. He also demanded a quality balance sheet reflecting no accounting games, and that the company operate with high integrity throughout the marketplace.

Most of the early HTI employees, both corporate and in the hospitals, were steeped in the family-oriented culture of HCA. The HTI culture that developed was a blend of that and the complementary management styles of Clayton McWhorter and Charlie Martin.

Clayton had long espoused the philosophy that employees work best if they act like owners. The ESOP gave Clayton the opportunity to push this belief, because all employees were, in fact, owners. The ownership structure at the outset had HTI management owning 10 percent; HCA through its warrants, 35 percent; and HTI employees through the ESOP owned 55 percent of HTI.

The formal structure was one thing, making it come alive was another. Paula Lovell was engaged as a communications and public relations consultant. Her creativity and common sense led to a series of effective communications campaigns, events, rallying points, and symbols that made the ownership culture come alive. Employee-owners in the hospitals and in the corporate offices developed a sense that "they were owners," and that whatever good or bad happened, it happened to everyone. Programs were rolled out consistently across all 104 hospitals and within corporate (e.g., "We Are Owners" buttons were worn until they wore out). A rallying cry was developed around the media reports that HCA had pushed off its dogs to HTI—employees became committed to "turning them into greyhounds."

Many stories were heard during those years about the positive benefits of the ESOP. In one case, a hospital maintenance worker figured out a way to extend the life of light bulbs in operating rooms. In another case, an elderly man fell out of his bed and made it clear he wouldn't sue the hospital because his niece was an owner. These are small things, but add them up across 104 hospitals and they helped to define a culture; it helped people stay focused on even small cost savings and making the business work as well as it could, just like they were owners.

PAULA LOVELL

President of Lovell Communications, Inc.

The ESOP was always more than a financing mechanism. HealthTrust stayed involved with the ESOP Association and used their research and information to help develop ideas for more "ownership" like involvement. The company developed financial incentive programs to reward people who acted like owners and found ways to make the company more cost effective and higher quality. I remember a maintenance guy who thought about how many times a certain expensive light bulb had to be changed in the O.R.s, and he determined he could change out the filament in the bulbs and it would last three times as long. The cost savings was calculated, he was rewarded, and he was written up in the newsletter for 23,000 employees to read about.

We celebrated the first five anniversaries of the founding of the company with themes and posters and collateral materials to reinforce the ownership mentality and the pride of ownership.

We made sure people understood their "stock" statements. Stock was new to a lot of people and there was some early mistrust. Surely it couldn't be as good as it seemed. We took pains to explain the statements through newsletters, payroll stuffers, meetings in the hospitals . . . so there could be more appreciation and a higher level of awareness about the value of an employee-owned company.

Another aspect of building and maintaining the culture was the annual management conference, which Clayton likened to a "big tent revival." This was an opportunity to bring together the CEOs, CFOs, and chief nursing officers from each hospital, as well as most of the corporate office staff, for a "little dose of HealthTrust religion." The meetings had a business side, an educational side, and an important social side to them.

The author tries to lighten up a HealthTrust photo-op in 1988.

Left: Paula Lovell provided the creativity for many of HealthTrust's communication campaigns. To build team spirit in 1991, baseball bats were engraved with the slogan "For a Home Run in the 5th!" Right: At a HealthTrust social function Clayton dons a disguise to better mingle with employees.

The credit for any success that HTI had is quickly shared with a lot of people who made the company work. Clayton remembers the important role Charlie Martin had in the early years.

I think one of the greatest assets we brought over from HCA was Charlie Martin. Nobody in the company was quicker at accessing a situation (even a twelve-inch-high stack of financial statements) than Charlie. I think one of the positives was having Charlie go over to HTI as the operating guy. My style at HCA was working through others and dealing with the big picture. I wasn't focusing on the details of all the hospitals, probably only the 20 percent that generated 80 percent of the earnings. It didn't take the regional people and hospital CEOs very long to know how Charlie's style was different and appropriate for our circumstances. He spent ten to twelve hours a day looking at *everything*. In fact, in those early days, Charlie looked at every account payable to be sure that we were buying correctly and that we were not overlooking any savings opportunity. He was also a prolific reader and came in many days with all kinds of new ideas.

The combination of the two executives' styles created an operating culture that bred intense loyalty and a focus on results. In HTI's first year, the efforts of other officers embraced the operating culture and produced the necessary results. Some notable cases include: Mike Koban in managing many of the relationships with the investors; Ken Donahey in implementing necessary financial and control systems; Bud Adams in managing the capital expenditures; and the five regional vice presidents of operations—Steve Brandt, Leon Hooper, Jim Dalton, Stuart Voelpel, and Jim Main—for getting their assigned hospitals on the right tracks. The management philosophy that evolved is perhaps best described with the four "guiding principles" developed to articulate it:

- HealthTrust is dedicated to meeting the expectations of those we serve by providing compassionate, quality, cost-effective health services.
- HealthTrust will operate in an environment of encouragement and challenge; innovation and continuous improvement; teamwork and collaboration; honesty and integrity.
- HealthTrust will provide leadership in the communities we serve.
- HealthTrust will conduct its business in a manner that preserves financial viability and creates shareholder value.

Word of HTI's initial successes received some attention in New York, and an interesting distraction occurred when HTI was barely one year old. In September 1988, Tommy Frist proposed a management led leveraged buy-out (LBO) of HCA at $51 per share. Shortly after this proposal was announced, representatives of Kohlberg Kravis Roberts & Co. (KKR) approached Clayton, Don MacNaughton, and Charlie Martin about helping them put a competing offer on the table. Clayton felt uncomfortable about the situation, but claims, "If someone comes to me with a business idea, I will listen." Several meetings were held to

Jack Massey (left), Paula Lovell, and Dr. Thomas Frist Sr. talk at a political function, 1988.

HTI going public in 1990: William Donaldson, NYSE and current SEC chairman; Donald S. MacNaughton; Clayton McWhorter; Mike Koban; and Glenn Davis.

explore the merits and procedures involved; however, KKR dropped their interest when they reached an agreement to merge with RJR Nabisco in November 1988. Since this merger was the largest corporate transaction up to that time ($25 billion), KKR's plate was going to be full and making a run at HCA no longer made sense.

IT WORKED

From mid-1987 to mid-1991, the hard work of thousands of HTI's employees produced positive results:

- Nineteen hospitals were sold to other owners. The proceeds were used to pay down debt, and thus reduce annual interest expenses. Ironically, the two El Paso, Texas, hospitals (Sun Towers Hospital and Vista Hills Medical Center) were sold to an industry newcomer, Rick Scott, and his startup company, Columbia Health Services.

- The hospitals that HTI purchased in 1987 had an EBIDTA (Earnings Before Interest, Depreciation, Taxes, and Amortization) margin of 12.8 percent in 1986; HTI's hospitals in 1991 had an EBIDTA margin of 20.3 percent.

- The net loss per common share (after preferred-stock dividends) declined from $2.52 in 1988 to $1.15 in 1991.

- Long-term debt declined 31 percent from September 1, 1987, to August 31, 1991.

- When the ESOP was terminated following the 1991 recapitalization, the annual contribution to employees' retirement accounts had averaged approximately 26 percent of their salary. This far exceeded the contributions of most company retirement programs.

The newspaper collage includes the following readable fragments:

MULTIHOSPITAL SYSTEMS

HealthTrust shows promise in firs~
executives prepare for future chall~

We're one year old
and proud of it!

By Howard Kim *Los Angeles correspondent*

Executives of HealthTrust-The Hospital Co. believe the company has come a long way since it began a year ago. The company has reduced its debt, sold unwanted assets, developed its own corporate identity and—best of all—made many skeptics believe that it can succeed.

"We have accomplished just about what we normally would in a year-and-a-half to do," said R. Clayton, HealthTrust's chairman and chief executive officer.

However, Mr. McWhorter is careful not to sound too confident. Despite the early successes, bigger challenges loom ahead for the still-fledgling firm.

Owner-operators. The mood around Nashville's corporate offices in Nashville, Tenn., is cheerful. The 96 hospitals HealthTrust has retained after selling eight of its original 104 ... also are nice places to work ...

tives and about 30,000 employees.
Efficiency campaign. From the outset, HealthTrust's biggest challenge was to increase occupancy and stem declines in patient days, chronic afflictions for the hospital industry.

During HealthTrust's first year, executives had little choice except to improve operating efficiencies. "We had the gun ..." Mr. McWhorter said.

... new hospital administrators ... brought in since June 1987 ...
HealthTrust officially became a corporate entity.
The corporate staff purposely was limited to 150—that's small for a company of HealthTrust's size, but the operation is extremely efficient, McWhorter said. While Nashville is the corporate base, five regional groups headed by their ... presidents oversee most of the company's operations. No longer overlooked. The ... are situated in 22 states ... South and Oregon, U ...

New hospital group ahead of debt payment schedule

GEORGE KEGLEY
BUSINESS EDITOR

NASHVILLE, Tenn. — The new HealthTrust chain of former Hospital Corporation of America hospitals at Christiansburg, Pulaski and 97 other locations is $169 million ahead on its debt payment.

The system of smaller and suburban hospitals, split off from HCA last September, raised $60 million from the sale of five hospitals and gained $109 million of unscheduled debt payments from operations, said R. Clayton McWhorter, chairman ...

Middle Tennessee, which is owned by Dominion Bankshares of Roanoke.

HealthTrust plans to attack the problem of unused hospital beds through joint venture leases to nursing homes, rehabilitation and mental health operations, he said. His company has about 20 possible locations for such ventures.

Although the company has some marginal hospitals, McWhorter sees a leveling out in the decline of hospital occupancy. Some beds have been shifted to day surgery ...

his challenge is to keep patients from leaving small communities for health care ... cially in the ... health care ... "We've got to slow down the out-migration of patients," he said.

In small communities, residents can receive certain outpatient services and procedures without having to travel, he said.

The new company's performance looks strong, he said. Among ...

A collage of articles, communication pieces, and management terms, circa 1988. This picture is from the commemorative book HealthTrust, Inc., 1987–1995.

JAMES E. DALTON

In a letter to Clayton upon his departure from HealthTrust
to assume the CEO role at Quorum Health Group, Inc.

HealthTrust has been rewarding, exciting, challenging, and a lot of fun. The shock of leaving HCA was offset very quickly by the people under the leadership which you and Charlie brought to HealthTrust. I know that I am a better manager as a result of these years at HealthTrust and I would not be having the opportunity to try my hand at a different corporate role if HealthTrust had not been successful.

The following is a letter to Clayton from a senior manager who was given a second chance to practice his profession at HealthTrust. This manager had been terminated from HCA a few years previously and convicted of criminal behavior. He convinced Clayton that he had turned his life around and could be a trusted and effective employee. He did not disappoint his coworkers.

Dear Clayton:

It is a genuine pleasure to be associated with HealthTrust, and I want you to know how grateful I am for having this opportunity. My family and I sincerely appreciate your support in making the restructuring of our lives possible.

Thank you, Clayton, for all that you have done, for your vote of confidence, and most of all, thank you for caring.

I am looking forward to working with you and assisting you in every way possible with the continuous success of HealthTrust . . .

THOMAS FRIST JR.

*This letter dated July 13, 1990, was prompted by an article
in a Nashville magazine outlining the success story that was
developing at HTI and Clayton's part in that success.*

Dear Clayton,

The July *Advantage* cover story about you and HTI could not have been better or more deserved. HCA, HTI, and the Nashville community are indebted to you for your many contributions.

I personally could not be prouder of your many achievements in such a short period of time. Just as importantly, you have realized your successes as a class act. Even your pictures (as well as quotes) come across as a conservative, confident, strong leader!

Clayton today gives most of the credit for the hospital performance improvement to Charlie Martin, the five regional vice presidents, and in turn, the hospital CEOs. They worked hard with a focused agenda to grow revenues, manage costs, and strategically position each hospital in their respective markets as best they could.

Even with good performance, the preferred-stock time bomb was ticking louder. Because of the "in-kind" dividends, it had grown 81 percent from 1987 ($319 million) to 1991 ($576 million). Refinancing was imperative.

An Initial Public Offering

On December 10, 1991, HTI went public selling its common stock on the New York Stock Exchange. The proceeds from this public sale of stock essentially took HCA off of the company's balance sheet. The preferred stock was redeemed and the financial time bomb defused.

Clayton's strategy of keeping the hospital management company analysts aware of HTI's progress paid off. Merrill Lynch and Co. was the lead bank in the transaction. Clayton, Mike Koban, Ken Donahey, and Hud Connery made a strong case for the stock, enduring the road show. The offering was successful and HTI was publicly traded. (Charlie Martin had left the company a few weeks earlier to pursue other opportunities.)

The process, however, wasn't without its hitches. Clayton remembers the night when the deal was priced and he was teetering between going ahead or delaying. HTI was hoping for a $14 to $16 price range, and Merrill Lynch said it would have to come out at less than $12 per share. Clayton told them that they would just have to call the deal off, packed up his briefcase, and headed toward the elevator. The bankers caught him before he got on the elevator and told Clayton they would try to make it $12. This required both Merrill Lynch and HCA to buy some shares. Clayton admits, "I often wonder whether I would've really gotten on the elevator and left the building or not. Twelve dollars was the minimum price to get HCA out of our financial structure."

Prior to the public offering, Clayton began broadening the representation on the HTI board. Vic Campbell (HCA's representative) had already gone off the board. Dick Hanselman had been on the HTI board from its beginning. He had a lot of experience on other corporate boards and was a supporter, but would not hesitate to speak up when something needed to be heard. About a year before the initial public offering (IPO), Bill Hjorth joined the board. He came with good managed-care experience, as well as strong financial credentials. After the IPO, Clayton continued his broadening of the board representation. Three additional outside board members were added, each bringing a unique perspective to the board. Bob Dee served on a number of other corporate boards and had been the CEO of Smith Kline Beecham. Harry Batey, M.D., was dean of the Northwestern Medical School, and experienced in the ways of having physicians and hospitals working together in an integrated delivery system. Alethea Caldwell also joined the board, having previously been the CEO of nonprofit hospitals and hospital systems, as well as serving a stint as commissioner for mental health in the state of Arizona.

Clayton picked every member of the board, playing out his belief that a board should have a healthy mix of experience and expertise—not clones or "yes" people. He balanced being friendly with each member, without having them become "captives" of his will. Clayton states, "This board did not hesitate to challenge me by asking tough questions or suggesting alternative courses of action."

RICHARD E. FRANCIS JR.
Chairman and CEO, Symbion, Inc.

When I became the SVP of Development for HealthTrust in 1992 our business strategy was clearly evolving from being a hospital company to a more comprehensive health-care services company. Given this dramatic shift in focus, it was essential that our entire capital allocation process mirror this strategy. So we began by conducting a comprehensive market by market assessment of our business. Our prioritization of capital spending focusing on three areas: outpatient service infrastructures; new service offerings; and acquisitions that strengthened our market position. A key contributor to the success of our efforts was that both development and operations had had a clear appreciation regarding the importance of coordinating our respective efforts. Therefore, the result was an ability to target our capital expenditures to not only make the strategic transition, but also insure that capital was deployed in a manner that met HTI return objectives. In addition, by prioritizing our markets in terms of type of investment, we were able to stretch our capital expenditures for maximum effect.

Mr. Outside

Throughout Clayton's career he has been involved in professional, community, political, business, and networking activities that are largely external to the company, division, or hospital he was running. He had a knack for bringing ideas, concepts, opportunities, and concerns back into his organizations. Often it would take the form of "food-for-thought," but there were many cases where some initiative was begun with the intention of doing something that would benefit the company. Looking back, a lot of frogs were kissed but a few turned into princesses. Four of these illustrate how this worked.

Tennessee Health-Care Exchange '90s (THE-90s)

In 1990, I was elected president of the Federation of American Health Systems. My goals and objectives for that year included focusing on health-care costs. I wanted to understand some of the health-benefit cost concerns that corporate America had for their employees, so I visited some of the trade associations that represented companies. My eyes were opened to the growing frustration of many companies and their lack of understanding on how to better manage their health-care costs. They said some unkind things about the health-care delivery and financing systems. For example, they felt the cost of health care was growing out of control due to over-utilization and the pushing of mental health services. It really became apparent that there existed a tremendous communication gap between all the parties.

I decided to try and do something in Tennessee. We pulled together a group of diverse people and different organizations from across the state. We had banks, labor unions, trade associations for business, travel agencies, manufacturing companies, large companies, as well as small. Our first efforts were directed at getting people together for informational sessions and discussions on different approaches for managing their health-care costs. We brought in nationally known speakers as well as managers of companies running exemplary health benefit programs. We had speakers that discussed the efforts leading to successes and failures of businesses, and the activities of community coalitions formed around the country for the express purpose of attacking health-care costs.

STEPHEN C. REYNOLDS

Then CEO of Baptist Medical Center in Memphis, Tennessee;
this letter followed the first of the statewide meetings
of the Tennessee Health-Care Exchange.

Dear Clayton,

The purpose of my note is to commend you for your leadership in developing our recent Health-Care Exchange. This was a "golden" opportunity for dialogue with key decision makers and you succeeded in my opinion as well as others. This concept needs to be carried forth across Tennessee and the United States and I will be happy to assist you in any way possible.

Again, congratulations for a terrific idea. It is time to quit complaining about our plight and develop solutions that make sense . . .

National Conference of State Legislatures, 1990: Clayton McWhorter; Thomas Frist Jr.; George Mitchell, former majority leader, U.S. Senate; Joe DiLorenzo; and John Martin, former speaker of house for the state of Maine.

The intentions were good and there was undoubtedly a lot of enlightenment. Unfortunately, when the time came for members of THE-90s to transition from an educational and brainstorming mode to an action mode, the momentum was lost. For Clayton, the experience did lead him to become a believer in the power of wellness programs to help individuals, and become a way for corporations and government programs to avoid or reduce health-care costs. This was the origin of the second initiative.

Wellness Programs

When Clayton was trying to better understand the issues of corporate America, he was asked a question by an executive from the PepsiCo Corporation, "How much does HTI spend on behalf of employees and dependents for sick-baby care that could have been prevented with better prenatal care?" He asked the question because PepsiCo had just analyzed their costs, and it was a staggering amount. Clayton brought the question back to HTI. He soon recognized that, not only was HTI paying dearly for inconsistent prenatal services, but their benefit program largely helped people who were sick instead of helping people prevent illness. He also saw that HTI had the same cost profile that most groups faced, namely that 10 to 20 percent of the group accounted for 60 to 80 percent of the costs.

What this created was a belief that it is prudent for companies to redesign their benefit programs to encourage healthier lifestyles, help people understand their particular risk factors, and build incentives to change unhealthy behaviors. So, HTI's health benefit program was modified to incorporate health screening through individual risk assessments, financial incentives to reduce health risk factors, and coverage for more preventive services such as physicals. Here is what Clayton says about the effort:

> The first full year of its implementation (which was the year before HTI merged with Columbia/HCA), we saved somewhere in the neighborhood of seven million dollars. We changed people's behavior and documented the savings. For example if you smoked and you joined a program to quit, your employee contribution to health insurance premiums was reduced. We had similar carrots built in for weight loss, prenatal care, and other risk areas.

Columbia/HCA acquired HTI approximately one year after the first full year of the program. The fledgling effort did not survive. Clayton recalls the reason given by Rick Scott, Columbia/HCA's CEO, "We're in the business to take care of sick people, not prevent illnesses." Clayton's own opinion was that such a perspective was short-sighted. Besides the social good associated with prevention and wellness, it ignored the fact that the company employed over one hundred thousand people and spent a lot of money on health care for them and their families.

Since his belief in wellness and health promotion was so strongly held, Clayton opened another door after the Columbia/HCA door had been shut. He worked with Yonnie Chesley and Keith Rye from HTI's human resources department to develop a company that offered these types of services and health plans to other organizations, and Gordian Health Solutions, Inc. was created in 1996.

HealthTrust Fellows Program

In 1992, a group of twenty HTI hospital executives (mostly CEOs) became the first of three cohorts of the new HealthTrust Fellows Program. The program was designed to take executives who were already successful in their roles and give them a learning experience that enhanced their leadership abilities and renewed their enthusiasm for leading their organizations. Jeptha Dalston, Ph.D., a seasoned health-care executive and educator, was engaged as the program director. Each of the three cohorts who went through the one-year program had monthly sessions of classroom presentations/discussions, guided homework, personal counseling sessions for career planning, and two, one-week field trips. The field trips were constructed to give each executive an opportunity to see health-care delivery from entirely different perspectives than what they see in their community hospitals. One of the trips was to London, England. The program involved two parts: 1) Classroom presentations/ discussions about the British health-care system, culture, and government roles; and 2) Each HTI executive was paired with an executive from the National Health Service and was able to "shadow" them as they went about their various duties. During the subsequent year, many of the British executives who participated in the London pairings came to the U.S. and visited their HTI counterparts at their respective hospitals. This opened a lot of eyes by seeing health-care delivery and financing operate in totally different ways. For example, HTI hospital CEO, Jerry Dooley, said, "I will never view home health care the same way." The second field trip involved a week paired with another health-care organization. The two organizations involved in this were the Henry Ford Health System in Detroit, Michigan, and Sutter Healthcare in Sacramento, California. The CEOs of those organizations, Gale Warden and Patrick Hayes, felt that their executives would also benefit from the exchange of ideas, perspectives, and experiences that the HTI fellows brought.

The program is an illustration of Clayton's beliefs that companies have an obligation to develop their people and that people need to "get out of their boxes." One way is to learn what others are doing. Larry Kloess was one of HTI's hospital CEOs (currently CEO of HCA's Centennial Medical Center in Nashville) who participated in the first class. He says of the experience:

> The HTI Fellows Program was a rare opportunity to examine management processes and decision-making in other organizations as well as examine our own beliefs. It was an incredible experience to exchange ideas with colleagues inside HTI, the Henry Ford organization, and the National Health Service. I learned so much from these colleagues, and have applied their experiences in a number of ways over the past ten years. There hasn't been anything quite like it in my career—both before and since—and the relationships formed in this program have endured the test of time. Even today, I look at the picture of my Fellows class hanging on my office wall, and remember the camaraderie of our group . . . it was a very rewarding experience.

The Peer Learning Network

Clayton had developed a relationship with Bill Trout, then president of Belmont University in Nashville. Initially this relationship developed because of Clayton's contributions to the school and his help raising donations from others. In early 1991, Clayton and Bill were talking about the fact that there was a lot of business talent in Middle Tennessee, and many of the companies had a lot of common issues, regardless of their business. They concluded that if Belmont could serve as the place where companies came together to learn and share best practices, all would benefit. They then met with a few business leaders to discuss the concept. Commitments were made and an invitation list prepared.

The initial structure included eleven Nashville companies: HTI, St. Thomas Hospital, Belmont University, Third National Bank (now

SunTrust), Opryland Hotel, Bell South, United Cities Gas, The Southwestern Company, Shoneys restaurants, Channel 5 television station, and the Ingram Book Company. None of these companies were direct competitors, each company identified five of their top people to participate, and bimonthly meetings were rotated so each company could play host.

The types of experiences varied. Sometimes world-class speakers such as Stephen Covey, Jack Welch, and Herb Kelleher were brought in; sometimes the larger group broke down into smaller groups to discuss issues and build relationships. Most meetings involved tours and presentations to help members understand the host business. For examples: Shoneys restaurants explained their bulk purchasing; Third National Bank showed how checks were processed; and Opryland Hotel toured the group around the "nonpublic" areas of the hotel (22 percent of the total space) showing the largest bakery, laundry, ice sculpturing, and meat-cutting operation in Middle Tennessee.

The Peer Learning Network has evolved and continues to meet. The initial objectives of education and networking have been met. Clayton sums it up:

> We have twenty-six companies today, and I think anyone that's been involved with this will tell you that it's been a good experience . . . I'm surprised when I walk in that room to see who is attending, it's a testament to its success. The important piece of all this is how people got to know each other—somebody would get up and talk about best case experiences, and then how open they were to anyone who wanted to come visit their shops, or let their people help them. We developed a lot of good relationships that we could not have developed otherwise. This was good for the individuals, it was good for their companies, and it was good for Nashville.

"Mr. Outside" can look back on these four initiatives (and others), and see the mark he has made on many organizations, not just the ones he was hired to run.

SUCCESSION PLANNING AND A LOOK
AT THE GOVERNOR'S MANSION

The initial public offering (IPO) was big milestone for HTI, the
Nashville health-care community, and Clayton McWhorter. Clayton had
been very active in community affairs and the Nashville business
community, and traveled in lofty political circles. His friend Ned Ray
McWherter was finishing his second term as governor, and Clayton had
been encouraged by many in the state to try and be his successor.

At the time, Clayton believed he could run HTI and be involved in
an exploratory campaign. He never declared himself a candidate, but
had begun laying a lot of the groundwork. He assembled a campaign
staff, visited forty of the ninety-five counties in Tennessee, and had
raised over a million dollars to finance the campaign. Interestingly,
Clayton, a staunch Democrat, had raised 30 percent of those funds from
Republicans, and the biggest single donation of ten thousand dollars
was also from a Republican.

NED RAY MCWHERTER
Governor of Tennessee from 1987 to 1995

Clayton had been a loyal supporter of mine for a long time. Jack
Massey and others had suggested to me that I tap Clayton for
advice about health care. I did that frequently. And, in early 1993
Clayton joined me and some of my supporters at a dinner. We all
thought he had a good chance to win the election if he got started
early and introduced himself around the state. So we encouraged
him to get a little more active and we would help in any way we
could. He did some "feeling around" and listening to what people
wanted . . . I felt like two of the big issues that the next governor
would face were education and health care. It seemed to me that
Clayton was knowledgeable and would have a head start on both
of those issues and could really make a contribution.

While he was "testing the waters," he was getting roughed up in the press. This, along with some inquiries from other companies and the stress created within HTI, led him to discontinue the process and return all donations. The distraction of this effort set some things in motion that proved to be pivotal for HTI.

During his campaigning efforts he began to get phone calls containing acquisition or merger overtures. Hospital Management Associates, a small hospital company from Naples, Florida, contacted Clayton first. Subsequently, American Medical International (AMI) approached Clayton with a merger opportunity. Also, Charlie Martin, who had become the CEO of Republic (later changing the name to ORNDA), contacted Clayton about an acquisition. These external overtures were one thing; the internal problems that followed were quite another.

One of the problems related to the question, "Who would replace Clayton as CEO?" Clayton admits that he hadn't done a good job with succession planning. After Charlie Martin left the company in August 1991, it was his and the board's judgment that other members of the management team were not ready to succeed him.

Not knowing the board's opinions, some members of HTI management ranks began speculating about who should be Clayton's successor. A few people began jockeying for position. At best, this was distracting, but in reality it was somewhat destructive to the management culture that had developed since 1987.

The board reassessed its support of Clayton's "testing the waters," asking him to reconsider his actions. They told him that there was not a successor in sight, and it was not time to merge with any other company. Clayton asked for two weeks to figure out what he was going to do, and that is when he decided to pull out of the race. He made the first announcement at a scheduled fund-raiser, which stunned the supportive crowd. The next day, Clayton announced his decision at a management meeting. Clayton remembers:

When I announced that I was staying with the company, it was obvious that some executives were disappointed with that decision. I was apparently closing the door on their imagined opportunities.

It was clear that I had created some animosity. I did what I could to heal any wounds. I even engaged a consultant, John Harris, who worked at Samford University to meet confidentially with each executive and try and help them work through their own issues. They needed to feel good about their roles and continue to perform for the company.

I felt compelled, however, to find a way to grow the company and show we were still viable and a player in the business. That's when I started the dialogue to acquire EPIC.

The EPIC acquisition brought thirty-one hospitals to HTI. Coincidently, these hospitals were structured as an ESOP, having been spun off from American Medical International (AMI) several years previously. An ESOP valuator was required to set the pricing, which came in at $8 per share. There was some controversy over this price—the EPIC shareholders feeling it was too low, and everybody else feeling it was too high. Nevertheless, the deal was structured around the $8 per share, and the hospitals were integrated into HTI's operating structure.

It was decided early on that the EPIC management team was not going to have a place in HTI. They would have been redundant to people already there, and Clayton felt like HTI already had the best team. The severance program offered to the thirteen top managers balmed their wounds and was considered generous. Some people began feeling that perhaps they would be financially better off if Clayton terminated them rather than staying employed.

In hindsight, Clayton realized he had underestimated the challenges of the exploratory campaign and continuing to run a young public company. He also feels as if an important opportunity may have been lost to HTI because of this distraction. During this time, there

Pledger L. Wattenbarger
Publisher & Editor

D. L. (Corky) Hoover
Executive Editor

"Freedom of the press does not guarantee fairness, accuracy or truth. It only creates the climate in which those things can be found from a variety of opposing viewpoints."

—Wayne Sargent, editor, 1984

CLAYTON MCWHORTER IS A RARITY

We have often written of political selfishness and abuse in this space, so it's a pleasure to take a different tact this week.

The opportunity has been supplied by Clayton McWhorter, an erstwhile candidate for governor.

The former Chattanoogan was little known among voters when he entered a crowded gubernatorial field.

He now lives in Nashville where he heads a health care firm known as HealthTrust. As a proven CEO and an expert in the health care delivery business, his talents could have been of particularly good use during a day when money is tight, and at a time when health reform is of such vital concern.

It was the matter of possible changes in national health care policy, perhaps, which prompted McWhorter to withdraw from the race in June, saying that business pressures did not allow him to make the race.

It was after he dropped out that he really set himself apart and above the average politician. McWhorter, who had raised over $1 million at the time, returned all campaign contributions to the donors. But, get this, he reached into his own personal bank account to reimburse contributors for the $150,000 his campaign had already spent.

This sort of action, ladies and gentlemen, is indeed a rarity. It says a great deal about Clayton McWhorter the man.

It makes us hope that we have not heard the last from Clayton McWhorter, the politician. We tend to believe that he would bring positive influence to any campaign.

was significant consolidation occurring within the hospital management industry. Columbia Health Services had grown to a seventeen-hospital company. Then in two extraordinary acquisitions, they acquired Galen (Humana's hospitals) and HCA. Tommy Frist, CEO of HCA, had already publicly declared that he didn't think he had the management team or the energy to continue growing HCA. This was confirmed in a private meeting with Clayton in October 1993.

Clayton's admits he did create some turmoil within the company at a time when it could have been more of a player. He admits that what he was focusing upon then was more of the political side. Interestingly, Clayton recalls that Donald MacNaughton provided him with this very criticism. All of this leaves the "What if?" question in his mind. Could HTI have been the player that consolidated one or more of these major companies?

PLAYING THE HAND WE WERE DEALT

The rallying cry of the late eighties for HTI was to turn HCA's dogs into greyhounds. By 1993, most of the hospitals were in racing form. Unfortunately, shifts in the growing market power of managed-care organizations left the rural, suburban, and often isolated HTI hospitals vulnerable to exclusion from necessary Health Maintenance Organization (HMO) and Preferred Provider Organization (PPO) contracts. Much of the hospital industry was consolidating into regional networks to provide "geographical coverage" and enhance their negotiating power with health plans. By themselves, many HTI hospitals were at a competitive disadvantage. Clayton describes the company's response:

> Our network development strategy was one where our hospitals that surrounded a metropolitan area needed to develop formal clinical and business relationships with some of the larger hospitals in nearby urban markets. Middle Tennessee was a market where we had twelve hospitals that referred largely to Nashville, some to Chattanooga. We began our discussions with St. Thomas Hospital in Nashville about building those

types of bridges. It was consistent with their own view of trying to solidify referral channels with hospitals outside the city. While this was going on, we acquired Nashville Memorial Hospital, and I think that created some difficulties with St. Thomas.

Some good initiatives resulted from the work between the HTI hospitals and St. Thomas. One such initiative centered on medical ethics. St. Thomas had an extraordinary physician who was also a lawyer and pharmacist. Perhaps it was the pharmacist connection, or perhaps just the good medical ethics program that Dr. Bruce White was running, but Clayton latched onto this and had satellite programs established in the Tennessee HTI hospitals and, later, in other regions.

JOHN TIGHE

*Then executive vice president and chief operating officer
of St. Thomas Hospital; now vice president of
Health Services, Corrections Corporation of America*

St. Thomas as a tertiary referral center was dependent on its referrals from smaller communities throughout Middle Tennessee and southern Kentucky. HealthTrust had the very institutions and medical staffs that were the lifeblood of St. Thomas. We were stand-alone and needed these referrals. So we viewed this network opportunity as something that would be mutually beneficial to St. Thomas and HealthTrust. What we ended up doing was to put together a natural network. Not based on ownership, but based on needs, based on interest in serving communities, and based on improving our mutual bottom lines.

Getting approval from the Daughters of Charity, our owners was huge. There were Daughters of Charity in fairly influential positions within the system that saw the for-profit hospital movement as the devil incarnate. Therefore we had to show that this relationship with a for-profit entity was really the best way of achieving the St. Thomas mission and ministry. We also had to show that HealthTrust wasn't the devil and that we really had more in common with them than some of the other faith-based and not-for-profit organizations in the area. It was an uphill battle.

We did move ahead with the St. Thomas/HealthTrust strategy and we began to see some of the fastest growth in hospital volumes that we had ever experienced. When Columbia/HCA announced their intent to purchase HealthTrust, we had a two-pronged reaction. First was dealing with "I told you so." From the system, from naysayers on the medical staff, and any one who had opposed our getting into bed with HealthTrust we heard, "I told you so." We had to deal with all that and not get overly focused on laying out blame and "what went wrong." Second, we had to do a quick regrouping. We were getting exactly the kind of business out of Middle Tennessee that we wanted. This pipeline was now in jeopardy and we had to quickly develop a new strategy knowing that there would soon be a natural relationship between the HealthTrust hospitals and Centennial Medical Center. Looking back, I am sorry the acquisition and subsequent ending of the St. Thomas/ HealthTrust relationship occurred, but it had the effect of forcing our management team to go to the next level. It got us far more attuned with how to get relationships and referrals regardless of ownership.

The work with St. Thomas Hospital was intended to help the Middle Tennessee hospitals and act as a laboratory for the networking concept. It was important that HTI understand how to build these types of relationships since it didn't have the wherewithal to acquire the large tertiary hospitals in many of the markets where it operated. It was expected that the type of success it was having with St. Thomas would have been replicated elsewhere. But the pilot program was cut short when HTI was acquired by Columbia/HCA. Any heartburn that St. Thomas Hospital felt over the Nashville Memorial Hospital acquisition was small compared to their reaction when their partner HTI hospitals became married to Centennial Medical Center in Nashville, an arch rival. Clayton recalls the awkwardness:

> The management folks we had been dealing with at St. Thomas and their parent company, the Daughters of Charity, felt like they had had the rug pulled out from under them. I visited Sister Almeda Goldson D.C., CEO of St. Thomas. She said, "I love you, Clayton, but I'm really disappointed by the way this has happened." And I said, "But Sister, I had no choice financially or legally once they got the price right." And she understood that.

But we are getting ahead of ourselves. There were some important events preceding Columbia/HCA's purchase of HTI.

THE DEAL BUG

Following the EPIC acquisition, the external overtures to HTI became more serious. The first of these suitors was National Medical Enterprises (NME). Their CEO, Jeff Barbakow, approached Clayton about joining the two-way deal between NME and AMI that was already approaching completion. The three-way arrangement would have created a ten-billion-dollar company, and it was serious enough that Clayton, Jeff, and a very small staff group explored the synergies; what could be eliminated, how the functions could be pulled together, and who would play what roles. During these early discussions, the valuations just didn't work.

Concurrently, Columbia/HCA was making inquiries of Clayton. They had submitted proposals which Clayton viewed as "low-ball offers." In the fall of 1994, the process got moving more quickly after a slipup at NME. Jeff Barbakow was preparing a speech for an upcoming annual meeting. He apparently prepared two versions, one based on the assumption of an agreement with HTI, one without. The wrong speech was sent to the *Wall Street Journal*. While this was embarrassing for NME, it lit a fire at Columbia/HCA.

Clayton was working with some investment bankers who were advising HTI and preparing for an informational meeting with the HTI board. Clayton was also relying on Carl George for much of the internal HTI analysis. By this time, Carl had proven himself a trusted and effective analyst and advisor. In preparing for the meeting, Clayton had concluded that his recommendation would be to do nothing at the present time. He prepared for the meeting by laying out the three distinct options:

> **Status Quo:** HTI could continue selective acquisitions, developing the business of each of its hospitals, continuing with the industry trend of integrated delivery systems, and working with managed-care organizations. Carl predicted that in the following year, 1995, the company would earn from $2.35 to $2.40 per share. At a fifteen times price/earnings multiple this produces a $36 stock price per share. He also felt that the company had sufficient free cash flow to meet its capital needs. On the downside, it appeared as though trends in the marketplace were working against the type of hospitals that HealthTrust ran. A recent Boston consulting group analysis of HTI's two strongest markets (Salt Lake City and Houston) suggested that they faced significant risks in their abilities to form or be part of competitive provider networks. Clayton also felt the pressure of merging HCA with other companies would not go away, but would continue to dilute management time. Clayton had been clear with the board that they would need to begin a search process for his successor, and internally, the management disruptions were getting worse.
>
> **Tripod—HTI/NME/AMI—Merger:** The tripod would make business market sense. One of the leading analysts, John Hindelong of Donaldson, Lufkin, and Jenrette, predicted that the market would reward such a merger and, in fact, the stock prices went up after the leak in the *Wall Street Journal*. The strategies of the

three companies were compatible, and NME and AMI were ahead of HTI in their efforts to integrate physicians and evolve into managed care. He also felt the HTI management group would have a larger role in the combined company than with a Columbia/HCA merger. There were some downsides to this combination. First, NME had already signed a consent decree with the federal government regarding various violations of the Medicare laws and regulations. Operating within those consent decrees would make decision-making much more frustrating and difficult. The deal had been proposed as a "merger of equals," and the exchange ratio would be less than that of an acquisition of HTI by Columbia/HCA. In doing such a deal, the HTI board would have to deal with the short-term and long-term returns issues and open themselves up for lawsuits. There was also a feeling that some of the controlling investors of AMI could delay the deal. This was enough of a concern that Clayton asked the investment bankers to look at an HTI/NME deal, excluding AMI.

Completing the Circle—HTI/Columbia/HCA Acquisition: The assets of the two companies matched up very well, and at a point in time when the industry was moving toward geographical networks, this would create a compelling story for Wall Street. If such a deal were to happen, there would be a higher premium than the tripod deal. Additionally, this would put the merger issues that have dogged HTI and caused significant distractions behind HTI management and the board. On the downside, the premium in the offer on the table was considered too low. HTI management would have less influence in the overall direction of the combined company, and there was some concern that the market might question Rick Scott's ability to handle another "big bite." It raised questions about how other hospitals in the industry would react . . . Would it cause them to resist this larger company even more or be driven toward it? There were also indications that Columbia/HCA hospitals were making a lot of independent deals with other providers in their respective markets. This suggested a shortage of controls and perhaps lack of organization in the quest for rapid growth.

While Clayton and the investment bankers were putting these recommendations together and preparing for the board meeting, Clayton received a call from Rick Scott and Tommy Frist. They wanted to sweeten the deal. They were now offering .88 shares of HCA stock for each share of HTI stock. The previous offer had been .85. They wanted a quick response, but recognized that the bankers needed a little time to assess this deal.

HealthTrust corporate management team, 1994. From left to right (front row): Jone Koford, Ernie Bacon, Beth Johnston, Ed Driesse, Yonnie Chesley, Hud Connery, Linda Hischke, and Mike Koban; (row 2): Parker Sherrill, Tom Corley, Ken Donahey, Larry Hough, Jim Fleetwood, Phil Wheeler, and Cliff Adlerz; (row 3): Clayton McWhorter, David Smith, Dana McLendon, Glenn Davis, Richard Francis, and Kent Wallace; (row 4): Rob Martin, Bob Vraciu, and Steve Blaine.

This was enough to change Clayton's mind. He went into the informational board meeting recommending that they accept the Columbia/HCA offer. He felt that if the deal were marketed properly, it would be of even greater value on a price-per-share basis by the time the transaction was completed. His recommendation went on to state that there were issues that would need to be addressed concerning how to deal with HTI's people, the Federal Trade Commission (FTC), receiving a fairness opinion, and reviewing Columbia/HCA financial information and documents. He stated, "I will continue to run HTI as I have until closing, and will keep you posted on any unusual matters." The acquisition of HTI was completed on April 24, 1995.

Justification for such transactions is often found in the business logic, the financial implications for shareholders, the improved market positions, and so on. Such deals also have personal agendas being played out as well. Clayton's reflection on those agendas for the three key players, Rick Scott, Tommy Frist Jr., and himself, is instructive.

I believe Rick Scott's motivation was just to keep getting the company bigger. That had been his agenda since he purchased his first two hospitals from us in El Paso, and this was possibly the last big acquisition the FTC would allow him to do.

Tommy Frist had lost the company headquarters to Louisville. HTI was the vehicle for getting it back. In fact, I had told him the only way I would do the deal would be if the company comes back to Nashville. Rick Scott was not really opposed to that since he had already burned a few bridges in Kentucky, and this was a way of getting out of there. The deal was struck that they would definitely come back and, as I have said before, after the price got right, and looking at the tripod opportunity, the Columbia/HCA price was a little better, the Columbia/HCA strategy was a little stronger, and Columbia/HCA's financials were stronger, so I figured I could be a player in the larger merged companies. The deal was good for the shareholders, it was good for the company, and it was good for Nashville. It would be the best of all worlds if we could pull it off.

I made a commitment to Rick Scott to do everything I could to get a tax incentive for moving the headquarters back to Nashville, but in fact, had we not gotten the tax incentive (and I couldn't tell the powers-to-be), the company would have come back anyway. We worked with the incoming governor (Don Sundquist), the outgoing governor (Ned Ray McWherter), the mayor of Nashville (Phil Bredesen), and the legislative leadership (Jimmy Naifeh and John Wilder) to reach an agreement in principle. The total package was approximately $126 million over a ten-year period. Both the Davidson County Metro Council and the Tennessee State Legislature approved the packages in early 1995.

NED RAY MCWHERTER

Clayton helped to arrange two meetings that I attended in Louisville to talk with Rick Scott about bringing the Columbia headquarters to Nashville. I flew up with the incoming governor, Don Sundquist, the Speaker of the Tennessee House of Representatives, Jimmy Naifeh, and the Lieutenant Governor and Speaker of the Tennessee Senate, John Wilder. On the first trip, the Columbia folks didn't want us to be seen, so we flew into Indiana, just across the river from Louisville and were taken to Columbia's offices. Clayton advised us on how to make our case.

After the board accepted the Columbia/HCA offer, Clayton remembers having to call Jeff Barbakow of NME. "I told him that I had agreed to a deal with Columbia/HCA. It was the shortest phone call I ever had with the guy. He asked, 'Is that final?' I replied, 'Yes.' He said, 'Thank you,' and hung up." NME and AMI went on to complete their merger and became what is now Tenet Health Services.

Even eight years later, one can't help but speculate whether accepting the Columbia/HCA offer was the best for HTI. Clayton is adamant though, "We did it for the right reasons. Our hospitals got into some strong networks, we got the right price, and we brought the headquarters home." He goes on to say that they could have survived pursuing the status quo. The market logic for regional hospital networks continued to unfold in most metropolitan areas; however, during the late 1990s, health plans lost some of their ability to exclude providers as corporate purchasers and corporate employees demanded broader-based provider networks.

HCA (after they dropped the Columbia name) has finally gotten the strategy they wanted. After spinning off Life Point and Triad, they are left with market concentrations of hospitals that are well positioned in their respected markets. HTI could never have had that. The logic of owned hospitals surrounding a metropolitan area and feeding patients into the larger city hospitals does not appear to be a strong strategy today. HTI's board did what was best for the hospitals; it was not necessarily the best for HTI's corporate management group and, as it turned out, it wasn't the best thing for Clayton McWhorter.

Financially, Clayton was not enriched by the deal. He didn't want nor did he receive any special considerations. At Columbia/HCA his salary was lower and he received no additional stock except for a small amount of options as an outside board member; the financial consideration to him personally was less than had he remained the CEO and chairman of an independent HTI. More importantly, after the deal Clayton assumed the role of chairman of the board at Columbia/HCA, and he entered his own personal "halftime."

PALACE REVOLT

As Clayton explains, HTI returned to the HCA fold for all the right reasons. The circle was completed. Unfortunately, not all members of Clayton's senior management staff agreed with the acquisition. For a number of self-serving reasons, they felt HTI should remain independent despite all of the market logic. It transpired this way:

> I [Clayton] was preparing to attend the University of Tennessee Board of Trustees meeting in Chattanooga. Before I arrived, I received a call from Don

MacNaughton, chairman of the executive committee of HTI's board. Without going into detail, Don explained that four senior managers had approached two board members complaining about the proposed merger and "about Clayton personally." I was stunned. I went through all the emotions a person goes through from disbelief to disappointment to anger.

I needed to act fast. I immediately called a few other board members to tell them what had occurred. I completed my phone calls later that night and the next day, and urged the whole board to attend an emergency board meeting. I didn't know how they would react, and I felt that it was important to talk to each one of them individually. I tried to contain my emotion and be states-manlike. . . . It was tough.

During my one-on-one conversations, I did not believe the directors had lost confidence in me, nor did I feel they were automatically defending me. They all seemed anxious to get the facts before determining whether the complaints had any validity. All the directors said they were surprised to learn that the executives had those feelings, particularly since the directors had met these managers on numerous occasions and never had any sense of dissent before.

The emergency board meeting was held on a Saturday and the whole board assembled, along with the four senior managers who had made the complaints. The managers were asked to tell the full board and [myself] what they had told Don MacNaughton. They started out by saying that they were opposed to the merger. I then insisted that they repeated what they had said about me person-ally. The story was that I: 1) procrastinated and was indecisive; 2) had a short fuse; 3) had no credibility with Wall Street, forcing managers to go out and communicate to the investment community; 4) that health care had passed me by; 5) that hospital facility managers had no respect for me; 6) that I'd created a lot of stress when I was thinking of running for governor; and 7) that I used business contacts to curry political favor. Was I stunned!

The board went through the complaints one by one. The managers provided no examples of my being indecisive or short-tempered, nor any convincing arguments on any of the other complaints. On the point about interacting with the investment community, one board member countered that it was flattering and beneficial to senior managers to represent the company to Wall Street. Such exposure generally showed Wall Street the company's management depth and gave the managers useful experience. The senior managers conceded that representing the company did have its positives.

Regarding Clayton's lack of respect in the industry, an outside director said he had talked to a number of HealthTrust's hospital CEOs at the annual management conference, and that they seemed to support Clayton enthusiastically. The senior managers reluctantly agreed that Clayton was well-liked. The outside directors then reminded the managers that Clayton was aware of the stress he'd caused during his political campaign and had brought in a consultant to try to help them with it.

Pressed on the point about political favoritism, the managers came up with one situation in which Clayton had given one of his big supporters a chance to bid on a project. The managers admitted that the person was a quality contractor and that the price was fair. It was the only example they could cite.

Following this fact-finding discussion, I excused myself from the meeting. Less than two hours later, the board called me back in. The board's overwhelming reaction was one of surprise that the managers were so dissatisfied and of disappointment in the way the managers raised the issues. The board felt that the managers should've talked directly to me rather than going around me to the board. Some saw it as a kind of arrogance and self-importance. A few of the outside directors chastised me for not recognizing the telltale signs of the dissent, but the board in no way implied that it was seriously considering having [me] leave and the management group take over.

The board continued its difficult task of evaluating the merger options and, as already explained, decided to pursue the merger with Columbia/HCA.

Shortly after the emergency board meeting, two of the four senior managers began changing their stories. They showed no regret and explained that they had been under a lot of pressure from their associates. As the backfilling occurred, more credibility issues were raised in the minds of the outside directors. The experience provided Clayton with a wake-up call and, as he often did, he reflected on what lessons could be learned. The first lesson related to board relationships.

First, I realized that I had not done a good enough job communicating with the board, particularly between board meetings. I was from the old school with boards, and always thought that the more you got them involved, the more you had to deal with them and the more they would try to second-guess your decisions. That kind of thinking is wrong. Since the palace revolt, I began dealing with the board differently. I began informing them better between meetings and they began participating more. The better-informed directors are about the business, the more quickly certain agenda items can be dealt with and appropriate decisions can be made. And they really didn't micromanage. Some board members have a tendency to get involved, especially in areas where they have expertise, but most of them are seasoned businesspeople who intentionally try not to get involved in the day-to-day stuff. I believe micromanaging goes on when the board members do not know what is happening and they have to start asking. Or it's an indication that the directors have lost a little confidence in the CEO and the CEO's lost some credibility.

I truly believe a CEO has a tremendous responsibility for good information, good overviews, and good reviews of the strengths and weaknesses of the key resources of the organization, including the people. Before, we basically presented financial information to our board, but we needed to do something more—we needed to show our real and more complete performance.

Capital needs must be understood so the board knows why you're doing capital formation, whether it's equity or debt, because sometimes you have to do it without calling a board meeting. The whole thing is to determine what the deficiencies of your board are relative to the business. What information did they need to educate themselves, but not get them into the mode of micromanaging?

The second lesson came as he contemplated the relationship between the board and senior management. He concluded that the board should have more, not less, exposure to management.

> The senior managers had been involved in board and committee meetings, but those situations were somewhat superficial. They didn't give the board a chance to perceive what was really going on. Now I encourage more informal exchanges outside the boardroom.

> I think it's positive to have management exposed to the board so directors can see the strength of management. For one thing, it is a critical piece of succession planning. I suppose some CEOs might be afraid that the board will find out something they don't want them to find out. My feeling is that the board will discover those things anyway. The fact is, if I'm doing something inappropriate, the board should have a means to find out. And the sooner they do, the smaller the problem, so it's to my benefit too.

The deal with Columbia/HCA was completed; the four senior managers completed their terms with HTI, and then went on to other business opportunities. It was an unfortunate footnote to another otherwise extraordinary business experience.

THE SPIRIT LIVES ON

The HTI experience is remembered by most of the former corporate employees as a "magical time." Nashville's health-care community is really like a small town. Since 1995, people frequently cross paths with others with whom they worked at HTI. In 2000, Clayton sensed the time was right for a reunion of sorts. He hosted the first at his house and was astonished at the turnout. Around 150 people took the time to show-up, catch-up, and in many different ways wish they could turn back the clock. After the first reunion, he committed to hosting future ones every other year. In September 2002, the second reunion was held with an even larger turnout and no less enthusiasm. The spirit does live on.

Chapter Three

HALFTIME

On April 24, 1995, Columbia/HCA completed the transaction to acquire HealthTrust. By that time, discussions about future roles had already occurred between the two management teams. As the acquirers, Columbia/HCA viewed virtually all of HTI's senior management team as redundant in the Columbia/HCA structure. This was okay since many of those HTI executives viewed the management culture at Columbia/HCA as incompatible with their own. Clayton did go over as the chairman of the Columbia/HCA board, thinking he would be able to play a constructive role. Unbeknownst to him, the buzzer had gone off—the first half was over and halftime had begun.

Clayton uses this sports metaphor because of a book he read in 1996, *Halftime*, by Bob Buford:

> I was reading the book and realized that I was in halftime. Halftime has nothing to do with age or retirement. It can happen in someone's thirties, forties, fifties, or whatever. It's when you realize that you are not excited about coming to work every day, no one is interested in your advice or counsel, and regardless of the salary, benefits, or all the trappings of power, you're doing yourself and the company a favor by moving on. How many people in this world are hanging on, working for somebody that makes them absolutely miserable? If you've got a choice and you find yourself in halftime, you need to move on.

Clayton was miserable! He described it as, "I found that I hated to go to work. They treated me like they would treat a grandfather, providing me with the typical creature comforts and benefits; but, they felt health care had passed me by, and they really didn't want any advice from me." For a man who had been guiding organizations successfully for over three decades, he found himself an outsider for the first time in his career. Three examples highlight how Clayton's frustrations grew.

In 1994 and 1995, an effort involving HTI, the Nashville business community, state and metropolitan government, and others successfully obtained $126 million of tax abatements over ten years from Davidson County and the state of Tennessee. This was the enticement for Columbia/HCA to bring their corporate headquarters to Nashville. Clayton opened a lot of doors and got cooperation from the leadership in the Senate, the House, the outgoing governor's administration, the incoming governor's administration, the Davidson County Metro Council, and the mayor's office. These efforts and having good relationships were minimized because Rick Scott wanted more. He convinced Clayton that he was ungrateful and not happy about the tax abatement program. He felt Clayton had caved in too soon in what were some "hardball negotiations" and he wanted him to go back for more. Clayton would not go back because he felt they had a fair deal upon which they had already agreed.

Rick Scott had not developed any relationships within the Tennessee or Davidson County political structure. Consequently, he was in no position to judge the deal's goodness. For example, the Davidson County Metro Council needed to approve their part of the abatement package. The proposal passed because of some hard work by Mayor Phil Bredesen and his staff; by staff from HTI; by lobbyists Cleve Smith and Butch Ely; and by use of Clayton's relationships with council members. The Metro Council's vote was an extremely rare unanimous approval (one abstention) of the abatement program.

Interestingly, Clayton recently spoke to Bob Corker who had been the Tennessee commissioner of finance during the negotiations for the state portion of the abatement. Even today, Corker confirms that, "it was a good tax incentive package," and that it went as far as the state would go. So, what had been celebrated early on as a great success got thrown back at Clayton as, "not enough." This is indicative of the difference in views of success and performance held by Clayton and Rick Scott.

Columbia/HCA was growing very rapidly. With the acquisitions of Galen (Humana's hospitals) in 1993, HCA in 1994, and HealthTrust in 1995, a seventeen-hospital company quickly grew to one owning and managing over 340 hospitals. The acquisitions themselves would have strained any organization, but especially a small company that just acquired three much larger ones. Clayton expressed his concerns about several things, including the absence of sufficient checks and balances . . . especially in the acquisition and contracting areas. This proved to be prophetic.

He was also concerned that Columbia/HCA was already too large to manage well. Clayton suggested to Rick Scott that he spin out a couple of groups of hospitals, selling off some assets. He likened it to a Baby Bell-type organizational model. Structurally, they would have some centralized corporate functions that could support the spin-offs without each having to replicate functions. The key was to get the operating units down to a size where there's no question that integrity and the quality of the balance sheet are maintained. In retrospect, Clayton believes that was probably one of the downfalls of Columbia/HCA's model—it grew too fast and they didn't have their hands on it.

The first Columbia/HCA board meeting quickly told Clayton that, "it was the Rick Scott show." As chairman, Clayton was allowed to open and close the meeting. In between, the meeting was run by Rick Scott.

Looking back on the experience, Clayton understands he misread the role he was to play in Columbia/HCA. While he is convinced he did the right thing for the HealthTrust hospitals, it was not a good step for him personally. In fact, he says he never would have agreed to be chairman if he had known how his role was actually going to work.

Clayton found it helpful to read the Buford book, *Halftime*, because it put in perspective where he was and what the next step needed to be.

When I realized I was in halftime, I started wondering, *Okay, what's in store for Clayton McWhorter in the second half?* I started thinking a lot about what

I was going to do. I began conversations with Rick Scott and Tommy Frist in January 1996 about my need to move on. I suggested to Rick that he ought to become the chairman and CEO, since it was clear that he really didn't need a chairman. It was agreed that I would step down at the annual shareholder meeting in May 1996, which I did.

I went through all kinds of emotional thought processes thinking about what I was going to do. Initially, I thought about a schedule which had me spending two weeks in Nashville, two weeks on my farm, two weeks on my boat, and two weeks at my lake house in Georgia, then I would start the cycle over again. But as I thought about what my mentors would say and what makes me tick, I soon realized that I'd be the most bored human being in the world if that's what I did in life. I felt like I still had something to contribute.

STUART MCWHORTER

Clayton's son, business partner,
and managing partner of Clayton Associates

I do remember [during Clayton's halftime] him being in a state of misery. I know that when the merger took place that the reason he stayed was the obligation he felt toward HCA and ultimately HealthTrust. So he stuck it out. But I know that the way the company was being led and managed made him feel like they didn't need him there. I think that bothered him because he felt like he could offer something, that he was still very active and he wasn't washed up. He could contribute and they weren't really taking his advice. They were asking his advice but I don't know if he felt like they were taking his advice. And that created this thought of being unwanted there . . . if he could go back, he would not have taken the chairmanship or would have relinquished it more quickly. The more he went into his office, the worse it got. I think that part of the reason was he didn't have something he could call his own. And, he's the type that wants to have that control and he wants to be providing something and doing something . . . at Columbia/HCA he just felt like he wasn't.

BRUCE MOORE JR.

Then senior vice president of Operations Administration,
Columbia/HCA; Bruce was one of many people who
had worked with Clayton over the years at HCA, HealthTrust,
and/or Columbia/HCA and felt appreciation
for the opportunity to work with him.
Many saw his retirement from Columbia/HCA as the end of a
working relationship that had benefited them in many ways.

Dear Clayton,

I wanted to drop you a note thanking you for everything you have done for Nashville, the company, and especially me over the years. I certainly hope our paths continue to cross but felt it an appropriate time with you retiring from the board to express my appreciation.

Many of us have been blessed growing up professionally in a company, community, and business environment that allowed individuals like me to observe the way you act and lead. Your support and kind words over the years have meant more than you will ever realize . . .

During this period from January to May of 1996, the *Tennessean* published an interview with Clayton. The article reported that he was stepping down as chairman of Columbia/HCA. Once word got out, two things happened.

First, Bill Trout, then president of Belmont University in Nashville, approached Clayton offering him an office and opportunity with the university. Clayton's relationship with Bill Trout and Belmont University had begun in the late 1980s when Jack Massey asked Clayton to make a financial contribution to the school. This relationship grew to involve Belmont's role with "The Peer Learning Network" and Clayton's larger contribution to fund the Gladys McWhorter Franks Multimedia Hall at Belmont University's library in honor of his mother.

The second thing that happened was that people began approaching him about business opportunities. One such discussion centered on assisted-living centers, and Clayton realized he could develop a passion for that business. A buzzer went off—the second half had begun.

Chapter Four

THE SECOND HALF

THE FIRST PLAYS OF THE SECOND HALF

C layton's mission in the second half has been one of giving back and making a difference. As the second half began, his game plan was still embryonic.

> I knew that there was something I wanted to do and the first thing was to go to Belmont and create the Center for Entrepreneurship. That began the process, but I wasn't quite sure where it was going to lead. I had made the decision to break away, knowing full well that I was not going to retire. That is, I was not going to go off somewhere and go fishing. I knew that I had to do something that was meaningful and significant for my second half, and in those first six to eight months I was flopping around trying to figure out what that would be.

Clayton went to Belmont University and started the Center for Entrepreneurship. He taught classes and helped to build relationships between the Massey School of Business and the Nashville business community. But he soon discovered that he could not be passionate about teaching. During this time, others came to him with business ideas and opportunities, and it was through this that his direction began to take shape.

> When the *Tennessean* published an article about me, you would have thought I had a big venture capital fund. A lot of people began knocking on the door

and telling me they've got a great business idea, and that they wanted me to help them start the company and help them raise the capital. I was approached by Alan Goldberg and Larry Sorrell, two former key people with Morgan Stanley Capital Partners. They asked if I would be a consultant with them, and I told them I wasn't interested in anything like that. We ended up discussing my interest in developing an assisted-living center company, and they said they wanted to work with me as a partner. So they became the deep pocket partner in the creation of LifeTrust and became a potential investing partner for other ventures.

Professor McWhorter realized that he needed some structure and an organization if he was going to do much in the venture capital arena and help people start companies. He created Clayton Associates as one vehicle. While this was happening, an interesting thing occurred.

Many of my friends and associates knew about my interest in assisted-living centers. They wanted to invest with me. Several of us met at Belmont one afternoon, and I told them that assisted living was a real marginal business and I wasn't sure how it was going to do. It seemed like the more negative I was about the business, the more they said that they wanted to invest. I had the sense it was almost as if they thought, *Clayton does not want us to invest in this because he wants to keep it all to himself.* Anyway, we allowed several to invest directly, but Morgan Stanley didn't like having all these different partners because it was too complicated.

To get around the complications for future deals, Clayton's friends and associates created an investment fund called Friends of Clayton Associates (FCA), which was designed to co-invest, that is, it would not invest in anything that Clayton Associates didn't invest in. Twelve million dollars was raised quickly to invest in other Clayton Associates ventures. Since this first fund, two other FCA funds have been raised. Occasionally, there are investments presented to Clayton Associates which the FCA advisory committee deems too risky. Then Clayton Associates may invest themselves or, in some cases, if Clayton has a passion for the business concept where he wants to help an individual, he will invest his personal money.

So the beginning of Clayton's second half was characterized by pursuing a direction rather than a clear endpoint, and being pulled into financing arrangements by people who believed he could continue to deliver. His cachet is described in the November 6, 2000, issue of *Modern Healthcare*, titled "Nashville Healthcare's Patron: In 'Retirement,' McWhorter Keeps on Building New Companies."

The name "R. Clayton McWhorter" is like the Good Housekeeping Seal for Nashville health care ventures . . . without McWhorter's role in the community, there is a good chance many of the health-care companies that are thriving today would not exist or would not be in Nashville. He provides an example of what one person's conviction and assets can do to shape an entire segment of a local economy.

—*C. Wayne Gower, then CEO of Iasis Healthcare Corp.*

They say the secret to business is networking . . . Clayton is the best networker around.

—*Richard Treadway, M.D., CEO, Medical Properties of America*

Some health-care executives have referred to him affectionately as the "godfather of Nashville health care."

BARBARA GARVIN
Director of the Center for Entrepreneurship
and director of Women's Programs

I wasn't surprised that Clayton put his talents to good use right after he stepped down from the chairman's role at Columbia/HCA. He collaborated with Belmont University and in 1986 set up the Center for Entrepreneurship where he could share his business experience with people interested in starting new ventures . . . particularly those who had less experience. He recognized that many women had good business ideas, but didn't understand the start-up process, especially regarding fund-raising. They also didn't have many business networking opportunities. With his support, the Center for Entrepreneurship developed women's programs that provided a forum for: networking, learning about legal structures, how to access venture capital, marketing, and so on.

CLAYTON ASSOCIATES

The "Godfather of Nashville health care" created the venture capital organization named Clayton Associates in 1996 to be an advisory and consulting firm for helping startup companies. The company initially began with just three people: Clayton; his son, Stuart McWhorter (part-time); and Bill Cook (a friend with over thirty years of business experience). It is with great pride that Clayton talks today about Clayton Associates. He is very proud of the organization that they have built, the companies they have helped start, and perhaps most appreciative of the opportunity to work with his son, Stuart.

Clayton Associates quickly evolved into a hub of strategic business development activities for health care and diversified service and technology firms, mostly in the Southeast. Their strength in networking and relationship building sets them apart from other venture capital companies. As Clayton describes it:

We're involved, we really try to help people; we try to network and we try to open doors. If a company needs to be doing business with hospitals, we call and introduce them and vouch for them. We use any relationships that we have to open doors, and that's one of the reasons we get so much attention and deal flow coming our way because we represent something more than just money. In some places we have a pretty good reputation, maybe in some places we don't. So, not only can we offer management advice and direction, but we can also connect many companies with other companies that can help them out.

Clayton Associates and its funds have made over forty investments in private operating companies. Most of the companies are in the health-care industry. The list includes:

- **Ardent Health Services**—behavioral and acute care hospital management
- **Auxi Healthcare**—home health-care management
- **Censis Technology**—surgical instrument inventory management
- **Community Care**—ambulatory surgery center management
- **Gordian Health Solutions**—disease management and prevention
- **HCCA International**—international nurse staffing and recruitment
- **HealthLeaders**—health-care magazine and online media service
- **HealthMont**—rural hospital management
- **HealthStream**—online health-care education
- **Iasis Healthcare Corporation**—acute care hospital management
- **Kelson Pediatric Partners** (formerly **Pedianet**)—pediatric managment
- **LifeTrust America**—assisted living and senior services
- **MedAssets**—medical asset management and group purchasing
- **Medical Properties of America**—health-care property management
- **Medical Reimbursements of America**—claims subrogation
- **Passport Health**—medical claims and transaction management

- Psychiatric Solutions—behavioral hospital managment
- Sodexho (formerly **Patriot Medical Technology**)—medical equipment asset management
- **United Surgical Partners** (formerly **OrthoLink Physicians Corporation**)—outpatient surgery centers

As Clayton Associates' investment portfolio grew, Clayton, Stuart, and Bill Cook saw three significant opportunities to add value to their portfolio companies and create a viable business in the process. First, most companies have particular service and technology needs that they will purchase from outside vendors. Clayton Associates has sought out or proactively helped develop a number of companies that supply those services and products, thus keeping some of those expenses (and revenues) "in the family." The list includes:

- **Ascendant Media**—online marketing and media
- **AT&T Wireless** (formerly **Tritel/Telecorp PCS**)—wireless PCS provider
- **Community Education Partners**—alternative education provider for urban school districts
- **Partners in Business**—provider of office product supplies
- **PayMaxx**—payroll processing
- **Place Collegiate Properties**—college/university student housing development
- **Smart DM**—direct and online marketing
- **Time Domain**—ultra-wideband technology provider

Additionally, Clayton Associates has invested in companies that serve as an affiliate to its core business of investing in private companies. These affiliate businesses are headquartered in Clayton Associates' offices to maximize the synergy and relationships. The affiliate companies include:

- Balentine & Company of Tennessee—wealth management, financial advisory, and consulting
- Cumberland Advisors—real estate development
- Dover Resource Group—business consulting, executive placement, and manager of a fifty-plus company consortium
- Harpeth Capital—mergers, acquisitions, private placement, and advisory services
- Medical Reimbursement Associates (MRA)—specialized accounts receivable company

The third opportunity focuses on the synergies that come from companies being in close proximity to one another. This led to creating a campus-like setting where as many of these companies could office "together." Clayton feels like he took the idea of Silicone Valley and applied it to the growing group of companies with which he had an involvement. That was the genesis of the Dover Centre in Franklin, Tennessee. (Dover was his mother's maiden name.) Clayton explains what he wanted to accomplish with Dover Centre.

> I wanted something that was sort of a campus-like setting. I didn't want a high rise, but rather something that would almost force you to run into other people going to your office. How many people do you see in a high rise? Typically, it is only those on your floor or people you see in an elevator. So that's what we built.

An underlying belief of Clayton's is, "if everything's equal you should do business with your friends, and if everything's not equal your friends understand why you can't do business with them." The campus concept of the Dover Centre allows management from many different companies to get to know each other. There are already many cases where resident companies have chosen to do business with each other because of those relationships. It is almost like Clayton found a way to put physical structure around the networking concept.

While good things have happened because of the active role Clayton Associates has played with associated companies, the people factor in the venture capital business remains the biggest success/failure factor. Clayton attributes their investing failures to the wrong management. It generally isn't the case of a bad business plan, but rather from management not being capable of keeping the company on course or taking it to the next level. So one of the big screens for business opportunities has become judging management . . . are the people credible, knowledgeable, experienced, have integrity, and possess the fire in their belly to get the job done?

Judging the management team may be the right thing to do, but it has cost Clayton Associates some money. Clayton tells this story:

> Before Jeff Arnold started WebMD, he ran a company in Atlanta that monitored pacemakers for cardiologists. He asked Clayton Associates to invest $400,000. Stuart and Bill analyzed the business opportunity and recommended that we make the investment. I said, "Absolutely not," because one of Jeff Arnold's associates was somebody I had run across while working at HCA, and I didn't have a good feeling about him. He was a guy that I did not want to be associated with. Well as it turns out, had we invested that $400,000 at that time (just before WebMD was created), that investment at its peak would have been worth about $50 million. Stuart and Bill often remind me of this.

It's not a surprise that Clayton Associates operates with a heavy focus on management talent. There are two interesting ways in which this has manifested itself. First, Clayton has always been the recipient of resumés from people who are looking, about to look, or just want him to know about them. At any given time he probably had more resumés than most executive search firms. A company related to Clayton Associates was created, the Dover Resource Group, which acts as a search firm and also networks people and companies that can do business together. They manage the referrals and mechanics of the processes. Clayton asked John Crysel to develop and run Dover Resource Group. John had been a successful hospital CEO with HTI and the CEO of Pedianet, Inc. (an early Clayton Associates investment),

Clayton and Stuart McWhorter at Clayton Associates.

which was later merged with Kelson Pediatric Partners. After this merger, John was "available" and agreed to pursue the concept. This matching of talent with opportunity illustrates one way Clayton Associates gains benefits from networking people.

The Dover Centre gave Clayton Associates another way to put some physical structure to networking and gain some benefit . . . it is called the "bullpen." Clayton gives Stuart credit for this concept, and describes it like this:

> We frequently see talented people who are between jobs, perhaps have been executives of companies that may have been sold, or perhaps they took a sabbatical and realized they need to get back into the work force. We provide a place for them to hang their hat, to use a computer and phone, and basically be present in our offices. We don't pay them, but they have a place to come and we allow them to participate in anything that we are looking at. If they want to sit in on a presentation, we allow that with a few exceptions. They see a lot of business plans and are exposed to new ideas. When you're in that bullpen you're going to see people all day long and somebody's going to come through while you're in the bathroom or the halls and say, "Hey, I would like to visit with you," or "I didn't know you were over here, I've got something you might be interested in." It's just the way it works.

So it's clear to see the value this has for the executive in transition. But Clayton is quick to say it's not just a one-way street.

> It's a valuable resource to have that talent pool around you as well. They need a job and we need management talent. They assist us in evaluating business models and management teams by attending our weekly meeting that covers new deal flow, business plan reviews, and portfolio company updates. This puts them in a strong position to start a company with our help or join the management teams of companies we see that need talent.

Clayton's day-to-day role with Clayton Associates has changed since his son Stuart joined the organization full-time in 1998. To people who know Stuart, it's clear this is not a case of nepotism. Stuart has earned his stripes in hospital administration with Greg Burfitt at Brookwood Medical Center in Birmingham, Alabama, and with OrthoLink, a physician practice management company, now part of United Surgical Partners. Stuart came to Clayton and said, "I'm ready to get involved with you at Clayton Associates." At that time Clayton was working with Bill Cook and a very small staff. "I tried to discourage Stuart, feeling that he would be better off continuing to work with somebody else, getting experiences from others besides myself." Stuart made a compelling case that he could make a contribution, and Clayton agreed. His comment about this today is, "I tell you, it's been one of the best things that has ever happened."

It's more than finding somebody he can trust who will do the heavy lifting on a day-to-day basis; there is the clear pride of a parent who is watching his son grow up and live the "right life." Regarding Stuart's role at Clayton Associates, Clayton says:

> He's really running the day-to-day operations; he's making tough decisions about what we will do, even to the point of deciding we're not going to invest in something. I might influence things from time to time because of my own experience. Or, I may say we're not going to invest with these people because I know their background and I'm not going to be in business with them, but by and large he runs the business. I've watched him grow by leaps and bounds. I'm not sure we would have done as well with Clayton Associates had I not let him become involved. Clayton Associates is in good hands.

STUART MCWHORTER

> What we've realized is that even though I am running the day-to-day affairs of Clayton Associates, and everybody knows here that I am the person in charge, as long as Clayton has an office here and as long as he's coming in every day, no matter what he's doing, as long as he's seen, people will forget about the fact that maybe it's Stuart McWhorter. Clayton has the ability to command this presence, and it's all out of respect. A business

consultant that we used was sitting in a group meeting with all of us, and Clayton was a little late for the meeting. When Clayton came in, the consultant noted how everybody suddenly shifted their body posture and they shifted how they were sitting in their chairs. He said he noticed that when Clayton sat back in his chair that people relaxed and sat back; when Clayton sat up and put his elbows on the table people kind of sat up in their chair a little bit and got a little bit closer to the table. That just speaks to the amount of respect that people have for Clayton. Not that they don't have any for me or anybody else here at Clayton Associates. Of course Clayton received that information favorably and his response was, "Well, how do we change that because we needed to change the perception?"

So Clayton has found a way to play the "gray hair" with an organization that's doing good things and doing them in ways that he is comfortable. He doesn't draw a salary and only owns 10 percent of Clayton Associates. He has set it up so that Clayton Associates will have a life of its own, and already sees the potential for its role changing. As investments become liquid, Clayton Associates builds its own investment pool. Perhaps down the road Clayton Associates will be more involved with mergers and acquisitions in companies that are beyond the start-up stage.

DRIVING FORCES IN CLAYTON'S LIFE

Clayton's "first half" was about career, accumulation, and accomplishment. This fits the pattern described in the book *Halftime*. His second half is more about family, giving back, and making a difference.

Family

An earlier section describes how important Clayton's mother, brothers, sister, aunts, and uncles had been to him in his formative years. Much of the time he was climbing the ladder at HCA and running HTI, he lived apart from his ex-wife, Angel, and their two children, Stuart and Jodie. While he made the effort to participate in important moments in their lives, that is different from being there day-to-day. He recalls the advice Dr. Frist Sr. gave him when Clayton told him he was getting a divorce. "The only reason you should miss your children's school play, graduation, or other special event is if you are a patient in the hospital, your car broke down, or your plane didn't fly. And, there will be times when you may have confrontational moments with your ex. Just remember when those moments occur, she is the mother of your children and your children will not appreciate her being treated unkindly." Clayton tried to live by this, and has repeated the advice when others have talked with him about their own situations. In such cases, Clayton sees signs of relief because he is not critical of them, and they appreciate the advice that has paid dividends to him.

This second half has brought new opportunities and a renewed focus on his family. Stuart moved to the Nashville area and works with Clayton on a daily basis. In 1992, Clayton purchased the Come Away Plantation, a 3,000-acre farm/hunting preserve in Georgia. He turned to his daughter, Jodie McWhorter-Coker, to make a business out of it. The operation has grown to approximately 4,400 acres (1,400 acres under lease for hunting purposes), and has added a conference center. This has given both Clayton and Jodie an opportunity to work together on something that they both love. Like so many who have worked with him, Jodie experienced Clayton's mentoring:

> I think that my involvement with Dad has taught me more than I could ever have learned elsewhere. His business leadership and guidance have taught me to look at the big picture and decide what I want to accomplish; and then to work my way backwards to understand what the first step should be in reaching that goal. I think the biggest contribution that my dad has made for me both personally and professionally is teaching me how to work with people . . . how to appreciate the good job that they do; how to get them to perform

and do the very best that they can do so that they want to work for me just like they want to work for people like Clayton McWhorter because he's kind, he's good, and he's fair. I'm his number one fan.

When he ended his seventeen years of bachelorhood and married Michelle (Smith) Jernigan, he gained a partner who has helped him learn how to enjoy life. He's been able to take more time away from work and travel—and he has even enjoyed it.

STUART MCWHORTER

Family was different pre-1995 and post-1995. The big difference was that Michelle had daughters and grandkids. It just brought a different element to his life. During the period when he was single, and living in Nashville, I was still in Atlanta. Until this day I'm still amazed at how often we saw each other. Now that I'm

Clayton shows off his favorite truck, a 1953 Chevrolet five-window pickup truck.

Daughter Jodie with husband Keith Coker in 2002.

McWhorter family portrait, 2001. Back row: John Bahur, Tyler Miller, Michelle McWhorter, R. Clayton McWhorter, Jodie McWhorter-Coker, and Keith Coker. Front row: Courtney Kline, Amy Bahur, Andrew Bahur, Matthew Miller, Kimberly Miller, John Austin Miller, Grace McWhorter, S. Clayton McWhorter, Leigh Anne McWhorter, and Stuart McWhorter.

at an age when I see the demands on an executive, and knowing that all he did was work, I am still surprised and amazed at how often we saw each other—at least once a month, maybe more. After he married Michelle, it wasn't just me and Jodie anymore; it was Michelle and her daughters, and now there are grandkids with more coming. I think he's beginning to see that through the grandchildren, how much joy that brings to him. Just like any grandparent, I think.

Giving Back

Clayton's mother instilled in him the need to give back time and money, even if you don't have a lot yourself. This was one of the basic values that he has carried throughout his life. Many charities, schools, his church, and many ad hoc causes have benefited from Clayton's generosity. People who worked with him knew that contributions to the United Way and political action committees were expected. Some viewed this just as a cost of doing business with him; others learned by example that giving back had its own rewards. Either way, charitable organizations wanted Clayton on their active donors list.

THOMAS FRIST JR.

Regarding Clayton's commitment to "give back," I haven't seen a real difference in recent years because it was always there. Everyone could see it. What I have seen after he escaped the umbrella of HCA and HealthTrust, is that he has more resources and time to devote to civic, community, and charitable type activities . . . I would hope that one of the legacies of HCA is that managers who worked there would step-up to their responsibilities in giving back to the community. Clayton was a wonderful example and role model.

A hunting party at Come Away Plantation, Norwood, Georgia.

The main house at Come Away Plantation.

In 1996 when the second half began, Clayton made a quantum jump in his personal commitment. He pledged to himself that he would maintain his net worth at its 1996 level and, "if the good Lord blessed me with some returns on that, I would give it all back, and I have." Since 1996, he has substantially increased his giving, mostly into education and human services organizations. These are just his direct contributions. In addition, he has served on numerous boards and fund-raising campaigns, being instrumental in raising "lots of money" from others in the community.

To date, the pledge to maintain his 1996 net worth didn't go according to plan. As the stock market rose in the late 1990s, the increased value of investments was either given away or pledged in multiyear commitments. The declines in the market since the first quarter of 1999 have eroded the base, and he is actually worse off than in 1996. There is no complaining or regrets. He did what he intended and that was to "give back in a more significant way."

Tom Corts

President, Samford University

As I think Colonel Sanders once said, "there isn't any wisdom in being the richest man in the graveyard," and Clayton surely believes that. I think the good Lord knew what he was doing when he passed out gifts and gave Clayton just the right ones, and Clayton has been a good steward of what he had to work with.

Aubrey Harwell

Lawyer, community leader, and longtime friend

Clayton's background is such that I think he understands and appreciates the public good that comes from leaders giving their time and their money to the nonprofit world. I think that being a self-made man as he is, and having seen what he saw when he was a younger man before he achieved great success, that he really recognizes more than many that you can make a difference, and he is committed to make a difference. Another reason he is so involved is that he can't say no to a friend. I asked Clayton to chair a Boy Scouts fund-raising campaign some years ago and he said he couldn't do it, he didn't have time, and I said Clayton, you need to do this, we've got 40,000 youth in Middle Tennessee and they're served by the funds that you can raise if you'll chair this, and he said he'd do it but he wanted me to promise that I'd never come to him again for Boy Scouts and I said I'd give him my word, my solemn word. It was a very successful campaign, he broke all records, and I went to him the next year and asked him to take over and be the Chairman of the Board of the Middle Tennessee Council of the Boy Scouts of America, and he said, "You promised me you'd never come to me again." I said, "Clayton, I lied. You have seen through the last year what a difference scouting makes and you need to do this." Needless to say, despite his schedule and despite the commitment that he wouldn't take on any new nonprofits, he ran the Boy Scouts for a couple of years and did a magnificent job.

RUTHIE SWIFT

Then president, class of 1990, Samford University; not only does this reflect the impact of Clayton's "giving back," but it shows how others benefit from this generosity and intend to "give back" as well.

Dear Clayton,

Last Saturday I walked across the stage to receive my diploma from President Corts, joining you as a member of the Samford University Alumni Associations.

I wanted to write and thank you for helping make my Samford education possible. Your gift to Samford University this past year helped supply teachers, books, and other resources that are necessary to a quality education.

My classmates and I owe you—and more than 3,000 other loyal Samford alumni like you—a debt of gratitude. Your gifts made a difference in our lives.

As the Class of 1990 moves on—to careers, to graduate studies, to places we may not ever know yet—I hope we will also join you as supporters of Samford University. Together, we will make it possible for others to benefit from Samford as we did . . .

AUBREY HARWELL

I think people who are self-made and are very successful and who have seen life from the perspective of a young person without any significant success, without any significant wealth, and then goes on to really achieve a lot, I think people like that tend to have a different view of what life is about. I think they tend to have a greater appreciation of what they have and a need to share it because they know what it's like not to have it. And I think that is part of what drives Clayton. But Clayton doesn't do this by virtue of any desires for publicity or pats on the back or accolades, as a matter of fact, knowing him as well as I do I suggest to you that a vast majority of his philanthropic acts, his charitable good deeds, are unknown except to a very small handful of people around him, because the things he does anonymously or almost anonymously are because they're the right thing to do. Not because it puts him in the public eye, not because he's in a spotlight for having done it, not because he's given accolades because of whatever commitments he's made. It's because he believes it's the right thing to do. And that's another core element of what Clayton's about. He sort of lives by that rule "do the right thing," whatever it may be. In business life, personal life, nonprofit life.

Making a Difference

When you ask Clayton how he's measured his success in "making a difference" during this second half, he has three outcomes that he proudly points to:

1. **Leverage the success and influence he has enjoyed for the creation of jobs in the community and wealth for the people who work hard to make that happen:** Clayton Associates has been involved in creating over forty companies that provide a needed service. Those forty companies represent 10,000 to 12,000 new jobs, and individuals throughout those companies have benefited financially to some degree. With each of those companies, there is a story about how Clayton personally and Clayton Associates collectively played a small or large role, and in many cases, made a material difference.

2. **Seek opportunities to serve as a mentor for as many young people as possible:** Clayton freely gives of his time and advice for young people who are facing situations and/or decisions about their future. He has benefited from the mentoring of several people along his life path; he not only wants to give the gift to others, but also have it multiplied. His only request of those he mentors is, "You can return the favor by being a mentor for as many young people as you have opportunity and always give back to the community which has benefited you so greatly." At first, some young people have disbelieved the pureness of Clayton's motives. Mark Vandiver (an executive with Balentine & Company, now part of Willington Trust Corporation) met Clayton at a Clemson football game and was invited to call Clayton's office the next Monday to set up a meeting. When Mark called, not only was he expected, but scheduled later that week. He recalls:

As I looked forward to the lunch, I must have contemplated ten possible reasons for his [Clayton's] interest in having lunch with me, and I was wrong on every count. After a brief discussion of my background, interests, and professional aspirations, our discussion was leading me to no apparent agenda. Finally, I graciously thanked him for his time and gathered the nerve to ask him what prompted his interest in me. He simply explained that he had no other agenda than a genuine interest in getting to know me and exploring ways in which he could be of benefit to my development.

Clayton did help Mark get established in his business and takes pride in his success.

3. **Helping people into college who would not otherwise be able to attend:** Clayton has provided scholarships and assistance in getting over twenty people into college. Sometimes it is the financial barrier that a scholarship can help overcome. Sometimes it involves making a call to the college or university asking them to take another look at the individual. While there may be some subtle pressure because a member of the Board of Trustees is asking, Clayton makes it clear that all he wants is for the case to be examined openly and fairly. He only makes these types of calls when he knows the applicant and often their family. Sometimes circumstances have led to poor grades, but the student is capable of doing well, and is ready and able to do so. Clayton follows their progress and gets great satisfaction out of their successes . . . no mistakes yet!

GORDON INMAN

Friend; chairman, Franklin Financial Corporation

Ninety percent of his calendar every day is for helping people. He gets a joy out of helping people, and that tells you a lot about a guy's character when their priority in life is helping people. He

doesn't need help from someone else, he's at a place in his life that he's happy, he's financially independent, and he's not interested in making a lot of money. He does it just to help people because I think that's his heart.

STUART MCWHORTER

Growing up like he did, he knows that there are people out there and all it takes is somebody to take an interest in what they're doing and sponsor them. He can provide some resources to help them, and when he says, "Let me know if I can help you in any way," he means that. He isn't just saying it.

January 2003 Easter Seals Nashvillian of the Year, McWhorter family: Leigh Anne and Stuart McWhorter, Michelle and Clayton McWhorter, Amy and John Bahur, Kimberly and Tyler Miller, (missing) Jodie McWhorter-Coker and Keith Coker.

HELEN KING CUMMINGS

Former senior vice president of reimbursement for HCA;
this letter was submitted and read during Clayton's recognition
by the Federation of American Health Systems, May 5, 1997.

Dear Clayton:

Congratulations on receiving the "Lifetime Achievement Award" from the Federation of American Health Systems. This is a well-deserved tribute for your tremendous contribution to the health-care industry during your career. It is always such a thrill to see someone such as yourself receive the recognition for making a real difference in the quality and availability of health-care services. Your dedication, talents, integrity, enthusiasm, and humor have been role models for us to follow.

Thanks for the influence you have had on my life. When I think of you, four vivid snapshots immediately come to mind. First, Palmyra Park was one of my assigned hospitals for Medicare Reimbursement, and it was time to prepare the first cost report. I came to the hospital to review the workpapers and met you for the first time. What an impression you made on me when you offered to help me measure the hospital for the square feet statistics when I discovered that the entire hospital had been measured incorrectly with the wrong scale by the controller and had shrunk the hospital about one-third! I knew that working on Medicare workpapers was not ordinarily the administrator's responsibility, but you demonstrated the traits at this early point in your career that led to such success by being a team leader, seeing that all the bases were covered, and using all the resources available to get the necessary job done which resulted in obtaining the proper amount of payments from Medicare.

Secondly, I think of your encouragement and faith in me during hard times. When I didn't get the promotion in 1975 to head up reimbursement for HCA, you counseled me to keep

doing my job with exceptional performance and the right attitude as the current timing wasn't right, but the door to my
future would open at the right time. You helped me to have
courage to take the Dale Carnegie course to improve my self
confidence. This helped me have the courage to negotiate the
settlement of the North Shore complex issues with millions of
dollars involved on the Medicare cost report for the management fees. I can still remember our conversations where you
would tell me that you would go with me to the negotiating
sessions with Blue Cross if I needed you. Knowing that I had
your support, I was able to have meeting after meeting and
resolve successfully this issue. Thanks for your encouragement
and for helping me grow so that in 1976 I did receive the
promotion and was much better prepared.

Third, I think of your philosophy which included risktaking
and tolerance level for mistakes. I was a perfectionist with
everything to be done 100 percent all the time. You shared with
me that it is all right to make mistakes but to learn from them
and not to make the same mistake over and over again. You
shocked me with your philosophy that an employee should be
terminated if he's right all the time as he isn't taking risks and
making timely decisions, passing opportunities while considering all the detailed facts. Yet, making decisions before enough
facts are available results in many failures and terminations of
the employee. You taught me that an exceptional employee will
have a success rate of 80 percent (the old 80/20 rule) to
demonstrate well-thought-out decisions considering the pros
and cons which is not *perfection* but *excellence.* Thanks for
helping me learn the difference.

Fourth, I think of the challenges we faced with the breakup
of HCA and the formation of HealthTrust. This degree of change
could best be depicted by the beautiful ocean wave on the cover
of *Forbes* magazine. This symbolic picture was representative of
your life during this time. WOW! How you conquered the wave

and surfed to fantastic success with the operations of HealthTrust, ultimately merging with Columbia/HCA, and becoming Chairman of the Board! Congratulations on a job well done.

Clayton, it has been my privilege to call you friend and mentor during these 25 years. As you continue your career through Belmont University to build young people's lives for tomorrow's future, I wish you fulfillment and success. I pray for God's richest blessings on your life. You have enriched my life, and I will continue to "pass it on" to honor you . . .

It would be an oversimplification to say that these three areas—family, giving back, and making a difference—completely define what drives Clayton. They do, however, reflect what he seems to value most at this stage of the second half.

Changing His Agenda

Although he's sixty-nine, Clayton is still energized, motivated, and looks forward to going into work every morning. He's made promises to his family to take one week off each month, and he's been able to do that. However, he admits that when he's away:

I'm calling in at least two times a day, getting my messages and returning calls. I get the messages because first, it's easier not to have all that piled up when you get back, but second, I'm afraid they're going to do something fun while I'm gone and I won't be involved.

So he enjoys what he's doing and is quick to add that, "When I get to the point where I don't enjoy doing this, I will quit. But I don't see that happening any time soon."

During 2002–2003, Clayton began unwinding most of his board commitments. Not only is it an impressive list of the ways he was involved, but it's clear that when he turns seventy in September 2003, he's getting ready for something else. Or is he? The list of resignations included:

- **Nashville Airport Authority:** He informed Nashville's mayor that he would not accept a reappointment or continue to be the chairman following the June 2003 meeting.
- **University of Tennessee Board:** He will step down in June 2005.
- **Board of Overseers of Samford University:** On November 5, 2002, he resigned as chairman of the board.
- **Tennessee Tomorrow:** In January 2003, he resigned.
- **Tennessee Business Roundtable:** Resigned.
- **Board of the Boy Scouts of America:** Will remain an honorary member of the board.
- **SunTrust Bank of Tennessee:** Will step down from the board in September 2003.

Whatever develops for Clayton in his second half, we can be comfortable it won't involve "going fishing." He's too energized by seeing the accomplishments of his efforts to give back and make a difference to walk away from the work that produces it. He's also steeped in the belief that "you must use it or you will lose it." After all, his mentors have worked well into their late seventies and early eighties. Thus, for whatever has been accomplished to date, one has to believe there is more to come.

Chapter Five

Take-Aways

Many people who have been successful in business and life want to pass on the lessons learned over their years. But, an interesting thing happens when you try to distill a life's worth of experiences into a magical list of success factors; it is very difficult to do it as an honest exercise. Clayton is the first to admit that many of the good things that have happened to him involved luck; involved being in the right place at the right time; or involved circumstances so unique to the situation that what worked for him at that time won't necessarily work for somebody else in different circumstances.

Having admitted to that, what follows is a description of four principles that Clayton feels are fairly universal. Each one ties to lessons he has learned during his journey.

Principle One—Find a Mentor . . . Be a Mentor

One of Clayton's first suggestions to young people is, "find a mentor, find a role model, and find somebody who can assist you in your professional and personal growth." Many people have influenced his life, so much so that his management style is a blend of the styles from many different individuals. A few examples illustrate the nature of these relationships and some of the important points he took away from those experiences.

"Dr. Olive was one of my professors while I was in pharmacy school at Samford University. I think he was one of my first mentors. He often warned us about cheating on exams. His favorite saying was, 'I know all the ways to cheat. So when you are in need of help, don't look to the left and don't look to the right . . . just look up.' So many times as I have made my journey I have followed Dr. Olive's advice and 'looked up.'"

Jack Massey was one of HCA's founders, after having been the successful CEO of Kentucky Fried Chicken. Jack Massey taught Clayton a very important lesson about *being prepared.*

> I will never forget when Jack Massey pulled me aside for a little one-on-one after I made a presentation to the HCA Board of Directors in 1977. I had recently been named senior vice president of operations and gave a report on domestic operations. I had figured that the forty-five-minute flight from Atlanta to Nashville was enough time to prepare that speech. Mr. Massey, in all of his infinite wisdom, had these words for me after that presentation, and they still ring loud, "Son, that was the worst speech I have ever heard presented to this board." About two months later, I gave my next speech to the same board. I rehearsed that speech not once, not ten times, but probably one hundred times. Mr. Massey was sitting close and he smiled as I came away from the podium. I have never forgotten his advice.

Another trait Clayton attributes to Jack Massey has to do with *being straight in answering questions and not stretching the truth.* Jack Massey had a reputation for knowing the answer to a question before he asked it. So, anyone answering a question by stretching the truth, shifting blame for something to somebody else, or trying to "blow some smoke," generally found a hostile audience. Clayton says, "It is best to admit that you screwed up or that you didn't know the answer to some question. Jack would counsel with you. He may not like an answer but he appreciates the honesty." This is sound advice for anyone. Eventually the truth will always come out, and you're much better for having been honest in the beginning.

Dr. Frist Sr. was the "spiritual leader" for HCA for many years. Long before the phrase "emotional leadership" made it into the management lexicon, Dr. Frist Sr. practiced it. He led people on an emotional level. He had a way of picking you up when you were emotionally down.

Clayton says, "I can't count the times he put his arm around me and said, 'Clayton, you're so important to this company, thank you for what you do.' Well, I don't know if I was all that good or not, but for the next two or three days, I could take on anybody."

Clayton took many things away from Dr. Frist Sr.'s leadership. He is quick to credit two aspects of his own management approach: "Dr. Frist Sr. was very fond of two sayings. First, *'Good people beget good people.'* If you're building an organization, you want to hire good people (capable in their job, but good human beings) in positions of leadership. They will find other good people to fill out the organization. Second, *'Don't lose your humility.'* Nobody likes arrogant folks. A little bit of humility can go a long way." This was imprinted on Clayton following a visit with Dr. Frist Sr. to the HCA hospital in Albany, Georgia, where Clayton started his career with HCA several years earlier.

> In the medical staff meeting, the doctors were getting up and saying how much they respected me, what a good job I did, and it almost appeared like it had been orchestrated by me. It hadn't been. Walking down the hall after the meeting, he put his arm around me and said, "You know, Clayton, those doctors really think a lot of you, but don't let it go to your head and don't lose your humility." I have never forgotten that.

Tommy Frist Jr. played a significant role as well. From the time he recruited Clayton to HCA until the day he left the Columbia/HCA board, Tommy was either involved or close by when Clayton passed a milestone in his career. They are kindred spirits when it comes to giving back to the community. They have been colleagues and, to some extent, competitors in the amazing business story of HCA. But what Clayton appreciates most was the opportunity Tommy gave him to take the leadership of HTI and grow professionally. Had it not been for his pushing in 1987, Clayton may have stayed in the safety of HCA.

Donald S. MacNaughton was a quintessential business leader. He had been CEO and chairman of the board of the Prudential Insurance Company and HCA. When he came into the HealthTrust organization as chairman of the executive committee of the board, he brought instant credibility. Clayton often thought, *When I grow up, I want to be like Don MacNaughton*. In so many ways, he brought professional management into the lives of the HCA executives during the late 1970s. Clayton recalls:

> He's one of those people who just had a presence about him. He was tall with silver hair. He could just walk into a room or through an airport and people knew he was somebody. He was very articulate, tough, and demanded excellence from people. In many ways, he taught me how to deal with corporate America. After all, that was his world for so long. I learned so much from him.

Donald MacNaughton stood for some beliefs that rubbed off on those who worked with him. He led by example and preached when appropriate about corporate responsibility and ethics. He was a believer that companies did not belong to top management but to the society that those companies served, and not necessarily just to shareholders. He had a knack for challenging executives to see the big picture. For example, he brought up the issue of the large amount of money spent on health care for the elderly where there was no benefit to a person's health or quality of life. Clayton recalls one discussion where Don MacNaughton said, "This problem will not be solved by health-care professionals. It will not be solved by government. This rationing question will be solved by society and religion." Clayton admits that he didn't fully understand the meaning until years later.

> Finally it came home to me that society is more and more accepting of an individual's right to avoid heroic medicine and even pushes people to set up living wills and advanced directives. It hasn't been too many years since doctors always did everything they could to give a patient one more breath of fresh air and even the thought of "pulling the plug" was criminal. Don MacNaughton saw this early on and challenged us to think beyond the walls of our hospitals.

Clayton's commitment to ethics was established before he met Don MacNaughton, but Mr. MacNaughton's questioning of such social issues was like putting gasoline on a fire. Clayton embraced ways to make a difference. He championed ethics programs in HTI hospitals and endowed the Center for Hospital and Healthcare Ethics at Samford University.

PAUL RUTLEDGE

President of HCA MidAmerican Division and TriStar Health
System; an operations manager with Clayton in the early 1980s

While I have many fond memories of working closely with Clayton, several things come to mind. He had/has a strong belief in the importance of mentorship. It takes time to include someone "in training" when the mentor has such an important and hectic job. Clayton found ways to "remember" me and I sat in many meetings that gave me insight into the world of executive management. While I learned significant lessons concerning management, I believe Clayton knew that the more I was involved, or at least informed, I in turn would be more useful to him in an assistant role. Clayton said often, "You're getting your Ph.D."

One of the more memorable lessons I received from working with Clayton was his ability to see compromise in issues that seemed pretty black or white. In many meetings, I would see Clayton develop thoughts or consensus around issues that weren't necessarily on anyone else's mind or agenda. I always thought if I wrote a book on management, I would base it a lot on my experiences with Clayton and title it *The Gray Flannel Suit*. Here's why, gray for Clayton's ability to find the "gray" in what appeared to be black and white issues. "Flannel" because it's warm and reflects Clayton's approachability by many people from all walks of life. And "suit" because Clayton is very much in the upper echelon of the business world.

No discussion about Clayton's mentors can be complete without mentioning Owen Brackett (O. B.) Hardy. Much of this relationship will be described later in the section entitled "The Coach on the Sidelines." The fact is, O. B. Hardy was Clayton's mentor and coach for over forty-three years. Through an incredible series of letters, phone calls, and face-to-face conversations, Clayton describes the nature of this relationship. "I now realize that O. B. Hardy accomplished a lot through me. He was calling the plays and I have just been carrying the ball."

These individuals and others had a big influence on Clayton's life and management style. Reflecting on this, he says:

> You've got to be born with some good genes to accept the direction and reinforcement that mentors can play in your life. But, I don't believe you are born with these skills. I think you have to acquire them; you have to be influenced by good people and learn the difference between good and bad. By the grace of God, I had the opportunity to live in a good environment even though we were poor as hell. I was influenced early on by my mother and throughout my career by a series of mentors. I guess I was smart enough to accept good advice when it was presented.

While Clayton is quick to give credit to others for important lessons accumulated over his life, he shows a lot of pride in the fact that he has been able to mentor and sponsor others, especially in his second half. When asked why, he says there are two main reasons:

> First, my mentors asked me to do it. They instilled in me the obligation that it's okay to receive, but you've also got to give. Second, there is a certain amount of satisfaction from helping others. It's similar to a teacher. Why do they teach? It's often for the satisfaction of helping others better themselves.

Many executives and managers who have worked with Clayton had some of his thinking and some of his approaches rub off on them. Perhaps the six people who worked with Clayton as "operations managers" while he was responsible for HCA's operations got the biggest boosts. Generally, he would identify a young manager with good potential and bring them into this role for no more than two years. In every case, the people who served in this role grew professionally, learned about HCA, and went on to establish their own marks in the health-care world. Joe DiLorenzo, Greg Burfitt, Bob Evans, and Paul Rutledge all went on to run HCA hospitals and assume higher operating positions in either HCA or Tenet (Greg Burfitt). George Garrett ran an HCA subsidiary selling hearing aids during the company's diversification phase. Scott Mercy worked as an operations executive during HCA's leveraged buyout, and went on to become the CEO of two other health-care companies before his untimely death.

Clayton describes the experience:

> They were a wonderful extension of me. They did homework for me, they did follow-up for me, and they screened information and would give me their recommendations or summaries of various matters across operations. They really helped me be successful. They were all bright, young people. It was a two-way street, however. They were getting a hell of an experience and education, but I was getting a heck of a lot out of them too. They all went on to do pretty well.

GREG BURFITT

Senior vice president for operations,
Southern states region, Tenet Healthcare Corporation

When I joined the company as an assistant administrator, there were only fifty-six corporate employees in Nashville, and Clayton had just been promoted to senior vice president over operations and was traveling a lot of the time. Eighteen months later, I was given the opportunity to become operations manager, a position I held from 1976 to 1978. The role was designed to be an aide-de-camp to Clayton and to perform special projects as requested for Tommy [Frist].

The functions of the job required me to become involved in nearly everything Clayton was involved in. It was my responsibility to make sure he had the information he needed when he needed it. I accompanied him to meetings and attended meetings on his behalf when he was out of town and completed multiple projects for him. I did primary research and interacted with others at the corporate office, including the officers of HCA, on a daily basis.

This level of involvement was very unusual because I was twenty-seven years old, and had been an assistant administrator at an HCA hospital and an acting CEO at another hospital for only a short time. I guess I must have stood out in some way, but I was nevertheless a pretty junior employee. The job was designed to last just two years, and to be a training ground for becoming a hospital CEO. It was possibly the best investment I could have made in my career in terms of experience, exposure, and maturation of thought processes. I had the opportunity to visit over eighty hospitals, interact daily with operational division vice presidents, monitor various legal and labor issues, handle personnel matters, and even make a presentation to the HCA Board of Directors. These were a very valuable set of learning experiences. Much of my foundation in terms of values and approaches to business decision-making was learned while in this position.

In order to make this role work, Clayton had to be very giving of himself, as well as very trusting. I wanted to work hard for him because he trusted me and believed in me, and one of the worst things I could do was to disappoint him. I learned something very valuable in that. There is no doubt in my mind that the people who went into this role were in fact honored to have that opportunity and were also mentored by him. Clayton taught, coached, and directed, but more often than not, I learned by watching, by doing, and by positive or negative reinforcement. Yes, this was possibly the most important professional experience of my life.

Paula Lovell

Infinite trust: For me, a distinctive mark of Clayton's management style is the gift of infinite trust that he rewarded me with. Because he was willing to trust me regarding media relations, developing communications strategies, and advising on crisis issues, I became ferociously loyal to him. Under no circumstances did I want to fail or lose his respect. On occasions, he would remind me that my firm would continue to have HealthTrust as a client as long as I performed well and earned the business . . . but we both knew that I was far more critical of our work than he would ever be. My goal everyday was to continue to have his trust and to continue to try to impress him with the quality of our work. On more than one occasion over the HealthTrust years, I worked through vacation days and even cut short a personal trip out West to return to Nashville and help with an important media issue. I never even told him . . . it didn't matter; the rewards were so great. There was something popping every day during those eight years . . . and when it was something new that I hadn't handled before, he didn't go out and hire another firm . . . he just expected me to learn it fast and get it done. I loved that about him. He was telling me that I was worth the investment in my learning curve . . . and therefore I always wanted to give him back 110 percent. In terms of my personal and professional growth, the value of all that was priceless.

Once Clayton entered the second half, there were far fewer opportunities for people to work with him in a business capacity and thus fit the pattern of a traditional mentor. So, in the second half, his efforts have morphed more into sponsoring others in their endeavors. Clayton will open doors, help people pursue opportunities, recommend people for something—essentially, play a big brother role where he can be there for somebody during an important moment in their life. He says, "Of all the things I have done in the later years, helping somebody get into school, succeed in business, or take my advice to stay on the straight and narrow, nothing else has given me so much pleasure."

Clayton really beams with pride when he talks about helping more than twenty kids get into college. In some cases, they had marginal grades or had messed around and didn't show well in the initial review by college admissions staff. This becomes personal since he really views himself as having been one of those types of students.

> I met a young man who had been raised by a single parent. This boy's uncle (whom I knew and trusted) wrote me a letter. He explained that the young man had applied to the University of Tennessee (UT), but in the application he didn't tell [UT] about flunking out of a school. When discovered, UT immediately denied his admission. When I read the letter from the uncle, it brought tears to my eyes. I investigated a little further. Then ultimately, I called an official at UT. I explained that this young man had made a mistake and I didn't think it was fair to penalize him just for making a mistake. He had been so ashamed about having to admit that he flunked out that he did what he did, and he realized it was a mistake. I believed that he needed a chance. I asked if they would allow me to fax the letter. Well, he did get admitted and has done very well. He works hard in school and works hard outside school in his part-time jobs. I keep tabs on him, and I truly believe he will be a productive member of the community. Now, I don't want this story to be interpreted that I can get undeserving kids in school. This is not the case. However, if I do believe that the kid will do well, all I ask of the school is that they give the application a fair hearing. Sometimes without a push like this, the application will never get looked at carefully.

A thank-you note from the boy's uncle captured the essence of Clayton's effort:

> I cannot thank you enough for the help you gave my nephew at the University of Tennessee. He was truly deserving of the second chance, and

you gave it to him. Obviously, many have the capacity to help others, but do not. Your reputation for helping others is well known, as well as the pleasure you get for doing so.

Clayton can help kids get with their college ambitions in part because of his long-standing commitment to education. He has served on the boards of three universities, building relationships and trust with their administrations. These relationships give him the ability to open some doors.

PRINCIPLE TWO—ACT LIKE AN OWNER

HealthTrust was an example where "acting like an owner" could be taken literally. The company's twenty-three thousand employees owned a piece of the action. They not only had a stake in their individual jobs, but a stake in how well the company as a whole performed. This ownership role, and the incentives it creates for people from floor nurses to corporate executives, was a major contributor to HTI's success. Clayton explains:

> You must act like an owner no matter what kind of position you hold in your company. You must think of yourself as an owner, not just an employee. You will get to work a little earlier and stay a little later. You will think of concepts, not mechanics. You will see the big picture and won't get bogged down in the details. You will make suggestions beyond the scope of your day-to-day assignments. And, you will start having ideas that will amaze and astound you and, probably, your boss.

So, the advice really has two thrusts. First, as an employee you individually ought to be acting like an owner. You will perform better and look better in the eyes of your boss, your boss's boss, and so on. Second, if you are in a situation where you manage others, a challenge is to motivate others in the organization to act like owners. The ESOP approach was one way. Profit sharing, stock purchase programs, and stock options are other vehicles for accomplishing this. But you've got to go beyond the vehicles.

People need to remember they are owners and see how they ought to be acting differently because of that ownership.

PRINCIPLE THREE—GIVE BACK

Clayton believes, "I have been blessed beyond my wildest dreams." Even in his youth when the family lived in poverty, Clayton's mother found ways to "give back." Later, working with individuals like Tommy Frist Jr., Clayton saw remarkable generosity and financial commitments to address community needs. It is no surprise that giving back has been and continues to be an important part of his basic fiber.

CHARLIE MANN
Longtime friend; executive vice president of
Surgical Speciality Instruments (SSI)

As Clayton rose through the health-care ranks I know his great friend and mentor Jack Massey always reminded him of the old biblical truth, "To whom much is given, much is required." He urged him to give back many of the blessings he had been given. Clayton has certainly risen to that challenge through his financial support of Belmont University, Samford University, the University of Tennessee, and many other organizations.

When one explores "why" he feels this way, it's clear that it is more of an emotional drive than an intellectual one. This comes through with a story Clayton once heard a minister tell during church services:

There once was a school that had a benefactor, a wealthy man who had made significant contributions to the university. These contributions came at a time when the university was struggling for its existence and the contributions helped it through those times and set the tone for success, which it did achieve.

Years later the administration wanted to honor this individual. They searched and searched until they found the once-proud old gentleman. Now, he was homeless—a shell of his former self. He had lost all of his material wealth. Because of his present condition, the elderly gentleman felt embarrassed to be honored. But he was persuaded, and was flown to the school where he was given new clothes and brought to the banquet that was being held in his honor.

He was asked to share his thoughts about what he saw on the vibrant campus. His words summed up his thoughts this way, "I thought I had lost it all, but I learned tonight that what you give away you never lose." Give back! Give back a little each day what you have been blessed with.

In Clayton's own words, this boils down to "the benefits you will reap will be in multitudes." He goes on to encourage people not to wait. Regardless of your situation, don't wait for ten years or until you've settled down or until you've achieved a particular salary level, and so on. It's not so much about giving back money as giving of your time, your love, and yourself. Whether it's to your family, your college, community programs, or church—it doesn't matter. Giving back benefits others as well as yourself.

PRINCIPLE FOUR—BUILD RELATIONSHIPS

One of Clayton's outstanding characteristics is how good he is at networking. He builds relationships with people in all walks of life and is quick to say, "You can't be an island unto yourself," and that you need to build relationships in order to be successful in business. To him it's more of an instinctive thing.

I don't know what it takes to make relationships tick. Sometimes they do, sometimes they don't. But I do know you have to work at it. You're going to do things like getting to know people, spending time talking, learning about a person's children, about their business, sending thank-you notes, returning their phone calls promptly, and perhaps just calling them to see how they're doing. The key is that you're taking time to get to know them and you're getting comfortable with each other.

At the heart of this is his belief that a business is part of a larger community. Other businesses are customers, suppliers, potential partners; there are elected officials that can help you or hurt you; there are community activities that bring all these people together.

The Peer Learning Network was one example of how Clayton personally developed relationships and, in the process, created a vehicle for others to do so as well. He was also instrumental in the creation of the Nashville Healthcare Council in 1994 as a focused effort by the Nashville Chamber of Commerce to develop the Nashville health-care community. Both of these organizations help many people network and build relationships within the business community. Other ways include one-on-one meetings and serving on boards of other companies and community organizations. These efforts can create opportunities to get advice, open doors, and get information about things that impact your business.

BARBARA GARVIN

Over the years that I worked with Clayton at HCA and HealthTrust, I saw many things in him. First, I saw a consistency in the way he felt about people. His dedication to helping others has followed him through every change we have made together. He has a genuine interest in helping other people succeed . . . helping them help themselves. Second, he forms great networks that not only help him, but by sharing his network, he helps others. Interestingly, this is how women work. They try to develop networks too. I think this may be a reason why he took an interest in women's programs. Lastly, with Clayton, there is never a throwaway. So many people will not help others succeed. And, if a person stumbles, there is the tendency just to replace the person.

Clayton will help the person who is stumbling get back on the right track.

Clayton is a big proponent of building relationships with political leaders, especially before you need to ask for their help. "That means you're going to go to a lot of bean suppers, you're going to give political contributions, you're going to develop relationships, and over time, the elected guy is going to have a comfort level with you." This was driven home by a longtime state legislator in Tennessee with whom Clayton had become close friends, the late Shelby Rhinehart. Shelby once told Clayton:

> You know, Clayton, the reason you get things done is because I don't have to do due diligence on you or research you. I know because of our relationship that you're not going to embarrass me, you're not going to come down here and feed me a bunch of bull, and get me to propose or oppose something where I might later find out that you had lied to me. If that should ever happen, you'll never get in my door again.

Clayton knows that if a total stranger approaches an elected official about some policy or regulatory matter, he or she is much less likely to get help. The elected official will need to check out the individual and research the issue. An established relationship can bypass a lot of that.

Shelby Rhinehart gave Clayton some additional advice on dealing with the state legislature. He said:

> Let me tell you something, Clayton. When you're dealing with the legislature you can't deal with all hundred of us because time won't allow that. Just remember we have a Board of Directors just like you've got a Board of Directors in your company. And that Board of Directors is going to be the top ten or twelve members of the leadership of the legislature, usually the speaker or the speaker pro tem, or the chairmen of the key committees, and government policy makers. That's the group of people that you need to develop relationships with. And just remember that how the leadership goes,

the rest are probably going to follow. So, if one of these leaders tells members of a committee opposing a piece of legislation that Clayton McWhorter is a good guy and he thinks we should reconsider the matter, there's a good chance they will. And the point here is that you don't have to go to every member of that committee.

As Clayton moved within the political world during the past twenty-plus years, Parker Sherrill was either at his side or never far away. Parker worked in government relations at HCA and HTI, and since 1995, has run a political consulting firm in Nashville. The two men made an effective partnership with Parker playing more of the management role. Clayton describes the relationship in terms of three things Parker has done—and done well:

1. **Director:** "Parker really prepared me for most meetings. He would tell me that I needed to know A, B, C about a person or situation, who was who, who I needed to see, and so on. For most of the relationships that I've built in the political arena, I have to give him much of the credit for keeping them going, for being sure that I followed up, being sure that I could get to the right people, all those kinds of things."

2. **The Go-Between:** "He's the one who communicates messages from me to many of our contacts. He's a master. He just knows how to use people and knows how to use lobbyists. He doesn't consider himself a lobbyist. He considers himself a processor. He knows what buttons to push to get something done as it relates to government relations."

3. **The Confidant:** "He can read the tea leaves in the political process and always tells me the truth as he sees it. For example, while I was considering running for governor, I bought a car in Kentucky. He told me to get those Kentucky stickers off the car and that I didn't need to be telling people where I bought it. He

asked why I bought it in Kentucky in the first place, and convinced me that I hadn't thought through things very well. He has taught me a lot about how to maneuver in the political world such as: 'You've got to think about this stuff;' 'Think about what you're going to say or not say;' and has helped me understand that if I take a particular position on something, it's going to get me in trouble later. He is very in tune."

So, the take-away is that individuals and companies will be better off if they proactively develop relationships with others. It of course involves time and money, and it is driven by a belief that "you cannot be an island unto yourself."

THE COACH ON THE SIDELINES

People entering the boardroom at the Dover Centre are often drawn to a large portrait showing Clayton and another man. Few people recognize the person with Clayton as Owen Brackett (O. B.) Hardy. When asked, Clayton is proud to explain that the gentleman with him is O. B. Hardy, his coach.

The relationship between the two men tells a story about Clayton as much as it does O. B. Hardy. Clayton is always open about the fact that many people have played significant roles in any success he has enjoyed. Having watched him in numerous situations, wrestling with big, small, and personal issues, there is a common trait: he seeks opinions, ideas, and advice from those around him—none more so than O. B. Hardy.

O. B. HARDY

Longtime mentor and friend;
former national health care planning advisor to Ernst & Young

The relationship began without a great deal of foresight. I had an able assistant [Clayton]. He was honest, loyal, truthful, talented,

and a workaholic . . . he did his job and a number of important
projects and was successful at all of it. You put all that together and
I could see he was going to be one of the people that I intended to
associate with. It's just that simple!

The relationship began in Clayton's first hospital assignment in
Phoebe Putney Memorial Hospital in Albany, Georgia. O. B. Hardy was
the administrator, and Clayton came in as the chief pharmacist. It
began as a traditional boss-subordinate relationship where the boss was
a teacher and developer of talent. It soon became something quite
unusual. Along the way, the two men became friends with O. B. acting
as a lifelong mentor and coach. In a November 3, 1998, letter to
Clayton, O. B. described to Clayton some of the health problems he was
encountering. The opening paragraph sums up a relationship that has
spanned over forty-three years:

> As you know, at certain times in your life I [O. B.] have written you letters I
> thought you might find helpful, and in several of those instances you have
> taken actions that made considerable changes that affected your entire future.
> I suppose there has been a father-son relationship between us of considerable
> strengths. I want you to know that I have appreciated that relationship.

A sampling of the content from some of the letters shows how a
mentor and a mentee can interact over a wide range of issues and time.
Also, O. B. Hardy has provided some sound advice which Clayton integrated, to some degree, into his own life. This advice might benefit
others. So, let's play voyeur.

Most people have heard the expression, "It is lonely at the top." Who
does the boss talk to about questions, doubts, and frustrations? Everyone
benefits from having one or more "sounding boards" with good judg-
ments. Clayton was fortunate enough to find a good sounding board, but
one that cared about him and provided him with unvarnished truth. Two
exchanges illustrate O. B.'s coaching role during difficult circumstances.

Clayton and O. B. Hardy

In early 1983, Clayton was executive vice president of HCA, and began to question whether he wanted to continue in that role, let alone aspire to a higher role. The two had already discussed the possibility of Clayton being promoted to president. O. B. provides him this counsel in a letter dated May 19, 1983:

> I realize that the position you have is very demanding and has been extremely aggravating at times. However, there are all sorts of problems and aggravations everywhere and, if I were you, I would not be thinking of stepping aside or even letting go of anything. The trick is to get yourself so organized and surrounded with knowledgeable and trustworthy persons that the thing will run itself. I realize that's easier said than done, but that is the right goal.

O. B. went on to explain that he shouldn't even consider retirement prior to sixty or sixty-five because of the terrible withdrawal symptoms a person has when they let go of power.

The reason that I know about these symptoms is that I went through all of it in leaving Phoebe Putney Memorial Hospital, and I have talked to a lot of others who found out about it when they reached a point where they weren't really a part of an organization and had no one whom they could order or instruct to go and do something . . . I sometimes get to reflecting on my shortcomings to the extent I think I'm not capable of doing much. The only way I can get myself up is to compare myself with the consultants around me. At that point, I start feeling better.

Clearly, Clayton stayed on with HCA, but the dialog continued regarding Clayton's situation. A letter dated July 28, 1984, offers some additional advice about matters the two men had recently discussed over the phone. They essentially related to the fact that HCA was beginning to struggle with earnings growth and the various non-hospital ventures operating under the HCA umbrella were raising new management challenges.

I realize you're grown and have a mind of your own, but when you're so close to any situation, there are some things you get caught up in which may not allow you to see as clearly as you would were you not so close. Had you been advising me over the past few years, I'm sure that you could have helped me. So, I don't think that I know it all; I know I don't, but what I am saying may be of some benefit to you.

When I was down there [in Nashville], you made the statement that you and Dr. Frist had always said that you were together and that if one went down, the other one would also. That has been fine up to this point. He has been your friend and has helped you immensely. Without him, you would not be where you are, and for that you should be eternally grateful. You cannot antagonize him, and, if I were you, I would always do my best to retain his friendship. However, in the event he has some problems with your board about policies for which you have had little or no responsibility, I certainly would not assume a do-or-die defense of him—not before that board. I would never kick his friendship in the teeth, but, at the same time, I'd not desert my chances to be president of HCA . . .

I'd be very careful about pushing [a senior executive] forward before your board. I'd let him take any heat which may come up from administrators who don't want to fall in line with the new processes, but I'd take credit for getting them started and for the successes which are sure to come from them. You have identified with Dr. Frist up to this point, and I think that [the senior executive] takes some pride in having bucked the hierarchy in championing market-oriented strategic planning and vertical integration. I would not let him take the credit due you for bringing these things about company-wide . . .

I mentioned this to you before, but I'll mention it again. I would keep line involvement in the formulation of policy at a minimum. Line persons have biased interests in any policy making, and you will seldom get objective opinions and answers from them. The outcome is bound to affect them and, therefore, they'll influence the outcome to what they think is their advantage. Or, they may influence it in a direction where they think they'll have the least hassle; the status quo is easy. Policy should be done by staff who have no conflicting interests in the matter. They should submit to you some alternatives which you may want some line people to review before you announce the policy . . . A fairly close analogy is this: airplanes are designed by engineers who may not know how to fly them—and not by pilots and other crew members. If they [pilots] were to design a plane, you'd have a cockpit twice as large as it is, as well as a spacious stewardess lounge rather than a fold-down seat.

During this time in 1984, HCA was beginning to feel the financial pressures of a changed hospital reimbursement system, investments in non-hospital ventures, further compounded by the effects of many hospital acquisitions. Board members were asking questions about the financial performance of the combined portfolio. All of this weighed heavily on Clayton and he was using O. B. Hardy as a sounding board and advisor for his own personal career planning. O. B. had told Clayton very clearly, "Don't resign, don't give up the prospect of becoming president of HCA. Plan as if you were preparing for the job and decide, if and when it were offered, whether you would take it."

A letter dated August 2, 1984, made it clear that the relationship between Clayton and O. B. Hardy had already become that of a team.

> I thought I'd send on to you some of my first thoughts about your forth-coming [speculating] presidency. I don't think any person ever had a greater opportunity than you. Frankly, I'd give my right leg to be in your place. Not being able to be there, I'll just be glad to give a few of my toes to help you. This is going to be the greatest fun we've ever had. Never believe for one minute we can't do it. You've heard me say a lot of times that there are some things I think, and some things I know. I know we can do it. All we've got to do is to do what we've always done: work hard, trust in God, and out-think the crowd. We're so accustomed to all that, it's just second nature at this point.

A letter dated August 9, 1984, laid out some steps O. B. felt Clayton should follow to improve his chances of being offered the president's position. They offer sound advice for others working their way up a corporate ladder.

> I've tried to put together some things which I believe will be important for you in getting the job as president of HCA. In thinking about these things, I've listed them in the order of my estimation of their importance. They're food for your thought and consideration and our further discussion.
>
> 1. Keep a strong hand at the helm until the actual appointment. Success in terms of profits and the exertion of strong leadership is imperative. In this regard, I don't think you have to do too much other than what you've been doing, but you've got to streamline your personal time and efficiency so as to make time for other things you probably should be doing.
>
> 2. Keep a close friendship with Dr. Frist and, as you said, make him look good. His unqualified support will probably be imperative. I also think that he wants you to keep a strong hand at the helm of operations plus the other areas of responsibility which you have.

3. Get the support of your board. A board usually admires somebody who can present well without being dogmatic and in any sense dictatorial. However, when and if you do present before them, know that you have your facts straight and know that you know the answers to questions which might be raised. There's nothing as destructive before a board as appearing that you don't know what you're talking about or to be presenting something which is incorrect in some way. This board will also admire the same things as Dr. Frist—success in your current position. Without appearing forward, achieve strong personal rapport with some of the members and hopefully a majority.

4. Keep the support of your immediate subordinates without relinquishing your control over them. However, don't dodge confrontations just to keep peace. If you've got a good reporting system going and give each of them some scheduled personal time each month, plus being accessible to them, there's not much here to worry about. Never circumvent them in the chain of command except in cases where you need something in their absence or in cases where you suspect them of hiding something which you believe is material.

5. Achieve high visibility throughout the corporation. I would not, however, undertake to visit individual hospitals in any way except in company with a division vice president and with the full knowledge of a unit president. I would make it a point to make timely speeches at meetings of division vice presidents, in company with the unit presidents. Also, I would present at meetings of administrators on a corporate-wide basis or on a regular basis, in company with the respective unit presidents.

6. Achieve public visibility on a national basis in the business world, as contrasted to [just] the hospital field. Basically, leaders in the hospital field can be considered, in a sense, failures. [Their] leadership image . . . [has] become "tainted" in the eyes of the public.

7. Enhance your speaking skills. If you think there's room for improvement, I personally would get some help. You don't have to worry too much about writing, for you can always get somebody to do that. However, I'd identify someone now upon whom I could depend for quality work.

8. Devise a protocol for most of the formal communications you make. And, don't be prone to deliver off-the-cuff observations; they can get you in trouble. In most instances where interfaces with the press are foreseen, I'd have a carefully worded written release ready.

9. Schedule your time on a formal, planned basis. Make ample provisions for your personal time. You are not going to be able to be everything to everybody even now, and much less so when you become president. Be firm in insisting upon seeing your subordinates when you should see them; take the initiative in scheduling them rather than having them solely looking for you. If one knows you have scheduled an appointment with him or her at a certain time, the chances are that seeking you at inconvenient times will be diminished. I believe you generally have an open door policy. This won't work from here on. You take the initiative of scheduling and retain the right to see most people at a time convenient for you and on your terms. If you don't, you'll stay overwhelmed with the unimportant minutiae and let slip attention to the first eight items I've listed.

10. Take positive actions to remain healthy. A healthy body promotes mental alertness and competence.

11. Maintain the overall air of a serious executive. In this regard, I don't think you need to change, but I'd be careful from now on what I said and to whom I said it. Many eyes will be scrutinizing you. Some will make a difference and some won't. However, there will still be some you think won't make a difference and they eventually will. I'll just conclude this by saying be very careful in all you say and do. Don't

let a little thing trip you up. You will have opponents and others who will be looking for something to hang you on.

Clayton followed this advice and did become president of HCA in 1985.

During the HTI gestation period, many people at HCA were nervous and a lot of "games were being played." Even Clayton was "in play." Would he stay with HCA or be "invited" to head up HealthTrust? Clayton and O. B. were discussing how to play it. In a letter dated April 28, 1987, O. B.'s advice included the following:

> In thinking about your problem, I don't believe this is the time for any type of confrontation. In fact, I would project an air of cooperation, except I'd not affect an air of enthusiasm for the transfer. Above all, I'd not confide in anyone (but me) your doubts, suspicions, dislikes, etc. Don't trust anyone with your thoughts. That usually comes back to haunt you. The very ones you think you can trust may have a direct pipeline to somebody else. . . .

> Here's the way I'd conduct myself on a day-to-day basis until issues are decided.

> 1. Be a statesman.

> 2. Be there, on the job, every day and project an air of being industrious. Deliver your best results.

> 3. Don't make any derogatory comments about any executive in any way. This doesn't mean you have to be out singing their praises.

> 4. If you do have to make the transfer, work to the best advantage of HCA until that day arrives. Then, take charge of the other company and run it to the best of your ability. I'll help you, and there are plenty of others.

> 5. Remember that situations come about from time to time over which you don't have a lot of control. Right now I would avoid trying to take

control, for I think that would reduce your chances of eventually getting control. Don't try to manipulate. Swing with the tide of events, and remember that good guys—not bad guys—usually finish first.

6. If you do have to take charge of the other company, you should be a company man. Every executive has an obligation not to develop any conflicts of interest. . . . Remember, around that place there are thousands of different interests and few are completely honest and truthful. . . .

Clayton was indeed chosen to be CEO of the spin-off company, HealthTrust. While there were tensions and conflicts as the terms of the transaction were worked out, O. B.'s advice was largely followed.

During the due diligence phase of Columbia/HCA's acquisition of HealthTrust, O. B. offered some insights and advice which proved to be prophetic. A sampling from an eleven-page letter dated January 5, 1995, provides a good sense of that advice.

First, I want to congratulate you on becoming the chairman of the merged Columbia/HCA and HealthTrust companies. As well, congratulations on your forthcoming marriage. I hope that both responsibilities will be highly successful. . . . You are coming into your position as chairman, however, at a time when you can make a real difference in the life of Americans. There are things that you can do to lead the way to a better day in health-care delivery. For whatever they're worth, here are some thoughts for you.

1. **Patients and the public first:** When the chairman of General Motors (GM) said, "What is good for GM is good for America," he was dead wrong. And, that man is remembered more for that goof than anything he ever did as chairman of GM. I will admit that I followed along when everybody started calling "service areas" by an industrial term—"market areas." But, that was a mistake with which we are all living. I now personally resent any health-care provider looking upon me or mine as a part of a "market."

Don't ever forget that you're in the business of providing a necessary, life-saving service to real people who hurt, who work hard, who scrimp and save to make ends meet, and in many instances, see their life's work swept away with one illness. . . . Everybody in the health-care field should be concentrating on providing optimum care at a reasonable cost to the public.

2. **Fraud:** One of the greatest surprises to me is the amount of fraud in the health-care field through falsifications related to charges. NME was really brought down by this and Charter Medical was threatened. Many others have been caught. Although I would bet that there has been little or no fraud at HealthTrust, Inc., I hope there is none at Columbia or HCA. As a first item of business after you get the job, I would see to it that there is no fraud going on. I would position myself so I would not be held responsible for anything that has taken place in either of these two companies, and if there had been improprieties in the past, I'd see that it was stopped and the causes for it and the methods used immediately eliminated. . . . Loyalty to friends is not a justification for any protection about dishonesty. The keys to success for this new company should be efficiency in operations, strategic positioning, appropriate service offerings, and correct organizational alignments.

3. **Accessibility to health care:** Every person in the nation should have accessibility to health care. Don't accept any posturing by Republicans that suggests this isn't possible or that we as a nation can't afford it. It is and we can, and in one manner or another it is going to occur eventually. . . . There are several possible solutions to affording total accessibility, but for now just let me say I believe you should take a posture that all should have accessibility in one manner or another. There has got to be a way. Politicians need to face up to it.

4. Insurance companies, HMOs, and other managed care organizations: Keep in mind that all of these have a non-value added status in health care. And, all of them interject a bias, one way or another, in the thinking of providers . . . I know, as a practical matter, that you've got to deal with what is existing. This doesn't mean, however, that what's existing is best, either from your company's standpoint or from the public's standpoint. Develop strategies that look to the greater efficiencies in universal coverage always.

The letter goes on with "big picture" advice on vertical integration, the future of health-care reform, positions Clayton should take regarding health-care reform, acquisitions, and his role as chairman. One interesting assertion is, "Community-wide wellness programs operated by each hospital should be a must, regardless of what you do about the other services I've named."

This advice about how Clayton should approach his career and his role was only one of the themes to be found in reviewing the letters O. B. Hardy sent to him over the years. Early in the 1980s, HCA, like hospitals throughout the country, adapted to changes in health-care financing and delivery. Clayton struggled with a number of questions such as, "How should HCA and HCA hospitals respond to these changes?" and "How should HCA analyze and assess its options?" and so on. During this time, O. B. Hardy was the national health care planning advisor with the consulting arm of Ernst & Whinney. During the period 1982 through 1985, there were many discussions and exchanges of letters and reports about such matters.

For example, the hospital industry began looking at diversification into various health-care services and increasing their emphasis upon the outpatient delivery of health services. In a letter dated March 18, 1982, Clayton turned to O. B. Hardy to help sort through some of the advice that he was receiving from various sources. O. B. played the role of the trusted advisor. He helped validate which of the many health services programs HCA should investigate for potential development and investment, including ambulatory surgery, alcohol and drug abuse programs, psychiatric programs, hospital-sponsored home care, physician office buildings, health promotion/wellness programs, etc.

Task forces, using protocols that O. B. Hardy had suggested, investigated the different areas, and a report with the final recommendations of the Alternative Delivery System's Task Force was prepared for Clayton's review and decision. Clayton shared this with O. B. Hardy, who didn't pull any punches in offering Clayton his assessment. After a point-by-point review, a letter dated February 15, 1983, contained the following comment:

> Clayton, you know Dr. Frist and Mr. MacNaughton better than I do, so you can better judge what they may think about this report. However, it only points at some possible directions. Frankly, I don't think that these line managers had any idea about how to go about doing factual investigations about specific things. Even in the case of home care and the regional laboratories, there's little documented evidence of what we might expect in terms of results. The recommendations are couched in terms of what I would call "unsupported generalities." I think you still are faced with getting some real investigations done. This work is for skilled staff researchers who should be located in the Center for Health Studies. I go back to my original comments to you. An administrator's job is to take action, which in many instances is in a fast-moving situation. He usually isn't trained to do research and beyond that, doesn't have the time to do it properly. Conversely a researcher's job is to ferret out unbiased facts, which is a thoughtful, deliberate process. An administrator should be given the researcher's facts and conclusions so that he or she can take appropriate action. I hope I haven't sounded too negative, and I certainly don't want to say we've got something which isn't worthwhile. However, the job is unfinished . . .

When the financial performance of the HCA hospitals began to suffer, a letter dated March 1, 1984, illustrates again how Clayton leaned on O. B. Hardy for honest advice:

You asked me to think about some things which HCA's hospitals should be doing to increase market shares in the areas where each franchise is operating. You're right—you can wring just so many dollars out of expenses and after that you have to increase business volumes on either or both an inpatient and an outpatient basis. To wring everything you can out of expenses it seems to me to be a mistake, for you're running the risk of reducing quality, both on a short-term and a long-term basis. . . . After getting your adminis-trators imbued with the fact that something has to be done about increasing business volumes, the next thing is to get them started off on the right direc-tion. And, the first thing that has to be done is not popular. A valid database has to be created.

O. B. concludes with, "Please don't take offense at the way I've expressed some of this. However, as you know, I've never striven for popularity, and I really believe that you don't want any self-serving expressions."

O. B. HARDY

My relationship with Clayton was more like a son to me than any other way that I can describe it. And there were some points along the way that this father-son relationship became more of a brother-brother relationship. But it was usually either a brother-brother, a trusted friend, or a son. Those three things right there spelled the relationship that I had with Clayton starting with a father complex in the beginning and developing into a highly treasured friend toward the end of it. We talked over the telephone a great deal.

This type of mentoring and coaching has gone on for over forty-three years. The two men still talk today, although there's less advice about advancing in a career and little commentary about the health-care system. How would Clayton had fared without O. B. Hardy? This is impossible to say. However, Clayton sums up this relationship in the following way, "O. B. was the coach on the sidelines. He developed the game plan and sent in the plays. I was just the quarterback carrying the ball." This leaves little doubt as to one of the main reasons why Clayton feels so strongly about people seeking out mentors and being mentors themselves for others.

CLAYTONISMS

Everyone develops their own philosophy of doing things in life and business, and Clayton is no exception. Below are ten that have served Clayton well and could easily be listed by those who know him. Clayton explains the meaning of each:

1. **When All Things Are Equal, You Should Do Business with Your Friends:** "First of all, it's got to be equal. If things aren't equal, your good friends will understand. That is, if your friends have a price that's higher than the competitor, they'll understand. On the other hand, if everything's equal, and you don't do business with them, they may not understand. This is more than a buddy-buddy thing. It's called networking. This networking can lead to support for legislation that is helpful to your company, it can open doors that lead to new business or access to capital, or it can get you extra service or fix problems quickly. Sometimes these benefits might even be worth a small price difference. In the end, you have to do what is right for the enterprise. I am just saying that evaluating a transaction sometimes involves more things than just price and that your friends can support you in many ways."

TOM RANEY
Senior vice president of R. J. Griffin & Company

Clayton's team building philosophy creates a turbocharged partnership that breeds loyalty and passion. He works with people and

companies that are good at what they do then goes out of his way to ask what he can do to help their business.

Clayton and I developed a friendship over 20 years ago when the general contractor with whom I was working had a team relationship with HCA. It was clear that our employees working on the HCA account were strongly committed to the client and eager to sacrifice many hours of personal time to pour their heart and soul into continually improving our service to them. By making us feel a part of his team at HCA, HealthTrust, and in other building opportunities, Clayton eliminated adversarial relationships and created an atmosphere such that people would run through walls for the common goal. His way of motivating us made us want to please him.

In the construction business, this interactive team approach allows our company, R. J. Griffin, to include subcontractors in the communication process thereby increasing the number of people committed to delivering a superior service. We have learned a lot from Clayton's management philosophy. Business relationships are like any other . . . by sincerely asking others how both sides can work together to improve results encourages people to respond with enthusiasm.

We can all learn from Clayton's example. If you want to build a strong following of people that sincerely care about your success, you better start thinking about theirs!

2. Be a Note-Taker: "There are two reasons for always taking notes. First, it jogs my memory. I usually only have to read one line to bring back a story. So, in some cases I don't have to write the whole story, just make some bulleted points. In other cases, I outline the key points and it serves as a record of what was said or what was agreed to. You'd be surprised how many times I've had follow-up discussions with people, and they remember things differently than what I remember. My notes give me the

means to refresh everyone's memory. The other reason for me to keep notes is that it helps me to be more focused on what is being said, rather than letting my mind wander."

3. **Managers Know About Managing Downward, But They Should Also Manage Upward and Sideways:** "I'm assuming that if you're one of my executives you know how to manage downward, because that's your responsibility. But, I believe for you to be a successful manager, you've got to know how to manage sideways, that is, your peer group. If you're one of the lieutenants on the management team, you've got counterparts. You may be heading up department X and they're heading up department Y. You have got to manage the relationship with the head of department Y because you may need their support or you may need to work out conflicts without going to your boss. This is essential to each of you achieving your goals.

    "Interestingly, very few people try to manage their boss. To do this right, you need to know what makes people tick—what are the hot buttons, what are the wrong buttons, and even what time of day to approach them. For example, I reported to Tommy Frist while I headed up operations at HCA. I carried around a list of things that I needed to get done that required his approval. Many times I walked in his office and he'd say something like, 'What's going on?' I'd just read the body language, and I might say, 'Just checking to see how you were doing.' Or, if the body language was right, I'd say, 'I need to talk to you about something.' So you need to be able to read a person's mood.

    "Also, timing can be important. For example, every afternoon Tommy would go out for a run. When he came back, he was generally on a high. I ocassionally needed his approval for critical things and would time my departure for when he was returning from his run. I would go out the back door of the corporate offices with my briefcase in my hand as he was finishing his jog. He'd typically say, 'Clayton, how did things go today?' We'd chit chat and I might say, 'Oh, by the way, Tommy, I've been thinking about something. I'd like to know if you think it's something we can go ahead and move on.' He would usually say, 'Yeah, that's fine.' Because of the runner's high, he was more open to things. Occasionally I got a 'yes' at the backdoor and the next morning he might tell me, 'Gosh, I shouldn't have said yes.' But he would always honor his word."

4. **Surround Yourself with People Who Are Smarter Than You:** "I have thought my job included motivating others and setting examples of doing things right, being honest, and operating with integrity. It's the leader's job to set that tone. But if you don't have people smarter than you, I think you've got a problem. At HealthTrust we had people who were very good at their individual roles, and they weren't a bunch of clones. We had diversity with people having different thoughts that challenged us all. People were able to make decisions in their areas without always having to come to me. I admit that I wanted to know what was going on, but that is different than trying to have me make all the decisions. I think the worst-run organizations are run by people who micromanage everything. For example, I'd frequently see people waiting outside Rick Scott's office at Columbia/HCA to get a nod or instructions. This slowed things down and often put Rick Scott in the position of making some decisions that were probably best made by others."

5. **Bigness Isn't Goodness:** "I don't know at what point big becomes too big. But to grow for the sake of growth creates many problems for companies. In fact, a lot of companies have gone bankrupt or missed opportunities because they got big through acquisitions and were unable to absorb the different cultures. Conflicts started occurring and management had to put out fires instead of building a culture for the new organization. I think that happened with Columbia/HCA. They quickly

acquired Galen, HCA, and HealthTrust, and had three or four cultures operating at the same time. The control systems became less effective, customers weren't being serviced well, and lots of things were falling between the cracks. This was a case where a big company focused on growing rapidly, but did not have its own house in order.

"I think that I lost sight of this danger when we were talking to Columbia/HCA about the merger with HealthTrust. When HCA had spun us off in 1987, it was, in many respects, wonderful to have an organization that was manageable . . . that you could get your hands around, and that you had some sense of doing a good job serving the public."

6. Get Out of Your Box . . . Expand Your Horizons . . . Be a Sponge: "When Don MacNaughton came to HCA he didn't have a lot of day-to-day knowledge about health care, so he'd ask questions. I remember him asking me why I was doing things the way I was, and I said, 'Because, we've always done it that way.' He'd ask, 'Why?' and then I'd say, 'Yeah, why are we doing it that way? Let's examine it, maybe there's a different way to deal with this issue, problem, or process.' Don would look at things at HCA from the insurance company point of view and force us to see what we were doing in a larger context. He helped us 'get out of our boxes.'

"By 'expand your horizons,' I mean learning from others. People need to seek out their own opportunities, but a company's leadership can also help. Very seldom do I have an original idea. I feel like I've developed a strength by taking someone else's idea and putting some meat on the bones to making it something more. Sometimes I listen to people talking and it triggers a thought. I try to take that thought and figure out how to use it. In many cases it might be easy just to ignore it because it might not have clear applications. So being a sponge is reading and listening, and taking your ideas and doing something with it. So that's just paying attention to what's around you, what people are saying or not saying, and learning from others. And that includes taking the advice that my mentors have given me.

"Now, in the eyes of some people this might be viewed as a negative, as if I am not smart enough to figure out everything without help from others; but to me it's like working smarter instead of harder. The key is accomplishing your goals and objectives. If somebody can provide ideas that you can build on or use, it is smart to use them; and when I've used someone's ideas, I've tried to give them credit. That is smart too, because they will be more inclined to share future thoughts with you.

"Companies can assist their employees in learning from others. We did a lot of that at HCA with the Center for Health Studies, and at HTI with the Fellows Program, and with the Peer Learning Network. We even took the HTI senior management team to visit Milliken & Company and to learn how they had won the Malcolm Baldridge National Quality Award. No one told us how to do our jobs better, rather we learned how others did their jobs and generated our own ideas . . . and there are ways you can facilitate this. Sometimes you can plant the seed [an idea] with others, and let that seed grow a bit. I can't tell you how many times a seed has been planted and a few months later somebody will come back and say, 'You know, Clayton, I've got an idea.' If it's their idea, the odds of it getting implemented are probably a lot better than if I told them that's what I wanted to do. So again, it's managing a process and managing a relationship."

7. **Don't Shoot the Messenger:** "I was recently at a board meeting of a company that encourages its board members to be candid. The chairman preached how important it is for us to be clear about what's going on, and that they don't need us as board members unless we are going to give them our best shot. That was the theory. However, in an executive session of the board, I

challenged something by saying, 'You've got a problem in this company. You're sending out mixed signals . . .' and so on. It didn't go down well. I was assured that wasn't the case, and that there were no mixed signals. Now, that's shooting the messenger. Fortunately, two other board members spoke up to say, 'Wait a minute . . . .'

"So shooting doesn't necessarily involve firing a person or something dramatic like that. It can come out of being defensive. You need to play poker and say something like, 'I appreciate that and I'm going to take it under advisement.' If you cut people off from telling you even small things, you risk never hearing the truth and not hearing about minor things that may lead to major things."

8. **It's Better to Ask Forgiveness Than Permission:** "You need to encourage people to take the initiative within appropriate boundaries. There has got to be balance and good judgment. I am not talking about giving forgiveness for someone violating company policies. For example, a company might prohibit political contributions to be made with company money and someone does it anyway. There would be no forgiveness and the individual would have to pay back the money. What I mean is that leaders need to encourage people to make decisions rather than always getting the boss to bless something. For example, if there are different ways of getting something done, go ahead and decide which way to go and do it. There should be a minimum of second-guessing and criticism for someone taking the initiative and getting the job done."

9. **"Choose a Job You Love and You Will Never Work a Day in Your Life"—***Confucius***:** "Unfortunately there are a lot of people who have to work to put bread on the table and they are miserable. They may be stuck because of the lack of jobs, or maybe their own lack of skills, or whatever the case may be. People who are

miserable in their jobs are not 100 percent productive. Even though they're going through the motions, they cannot wait until five o'clock, they can't wait for lunchtime to come, they hate their boss, and all those things. It's like a bad marriage; it's a terrible situation, but some stay in it because they've got children. And a person may stay in the bad job because he doesn't have other options. Okay, that's a fact. And there are a lot of people in this world in that situation.

"I am talking about people who can take the initiative and who can see an opportunity. Consider taking the risk and making changes even though there are short-term consequences—your life can be a lot better. Let me give you an example. Tyler Miller, my son-in-law, recently left Ingram Industries. Tyler felt it was time to go, so he began to look around. He had two or three opportunities which we discussed. I told him, 'I haven't done any due diligence on the opportunities, but let me ask you some questions. Of the key people involved in the three opportunities, which ones do you feel have the most integrity? Which ones have been above board with you?' The next thing I said was, 'Forget the salaries, no one has ever gotten wealthy off of a salary. The only way you can create wealth is to get a multiple of something. What's going to really excite you every morning, every waking hour, of these three opportunities?' He made his decision and then told me why. The person he chose to work with was honest, they were able to obtain financial backing, and Tyler saw an opportunity to complement her skills. Now you're talking about a guy that's pumped up! He's found a job he loves."

10. **Volunteer for Projects:** "Why volunteer? Well, it's paying the price, it's getting exposure. There are a lot of good people in this world. There are a lot of good human resources within a company, but the boss or decision makers won't know about them unless they've got a good sponsor. A good way to get

exposure is to do things that go above and beyond. Volunteer for projects that can help you stand out in constructive ways. That's what this is about. When I started getting involved in the political process, I wasn't too interested in going to bean suppers or political events. But doing so gave me exposure . . . it gave me some power or influence because the relationships I built became important to the organization. People began to depend on me to provide access to certain people. But you have to go above and beyond to do it. And then over time it just sort of evolves. You know, now I like it. It almost has become a way of life."

S everal people who know Clayton well have commented on Clayton's gift for making others feels special. Here is what they had to say:

JOHN HALEY
Longtime friend; chairman of Southeastern Telecom

I noticed that it doesn't make any difference who comes up and talks to him at whatever function, or whatever ball game, or whatever get-together. He gives them eye contact, he listens to them, and he's there to help them if he can. It doesn't make any difference who it is . . . He is sincerely humble . . . And everybody that I've introduced Clayton to has this picture of this guy that has made all this money, has risen to all this success in the business world, and you mean he's nice? He's really a nice guy and is a man without a tremendous ego.

CHARLIE MANN

You would never know that he has reached the pinnacle of life that he has reached today because it doesn't matter if you're somebody, a janitor at a hospital or the CEO of a large corporation. He treats everybody the same and makes you feel good . . . when he talks to you he looks you straight in the eye and makes you feel like you're the most important person at the moment when he is talking to you. He doesn't get distracted by anybody else . . . he just makes you feel good.

RUDY RUARK

Longtime friend; vice president of Commerce Capital

I just think he likes to see other people do well and help the community. He's a very amiable person, he's really into making other people feel good, and that's why I think he can walk in a room and make you feel very at home. It's not his agenda to see what he can get out of your pocket. He cares about you as a person.

GORDON INMAN

He has the ability to put himself on the same level with that person. And that's a gift, and that's one reason everybody likes him. Clayton McWhorter can talk to the president of the United States, or he can talk to the biggest redneck in Tennessee, and he can make either one of those people very, very comfortable and feel good . . . he doesn't forget where he came from.

AUBREY HARWELL

Clayton McWhorter has achieved phenomenal success in the business world; he has been honored more times than I care to think about in the nonprofit world. In spite of all that, he is totally and completely lacking in arrogance. He's one of those rare people that treats everybody the same—from the valet parker to a server at a restaurant to the president of the United States. Clayton McWhorter treats everybody with kindness and with respect, with fundamental decency, and I think people react to that. I think people tend to appreciate the fact that he has achieved a great deal of success but he does not manifest aloofness or arrogance or self-pride.

STUART MCWHORTER

I believe that the most important thing is the golden rule in that he treats people with respect and dignity and integrity, and that he surely is dealing with people or situations from his heart . . . he truly deals with people because he cares about the person and he wants to do the right thing. But I also feel that part of it is that somebody of his stature and with the success he's had, the fact that he can deal with people on an individual basis, he listens to them, he looks them in the eye, he takes every single word in somebody says to him, and I've heard many times people come up to me after they meet Clayton for the first time and they just can't believe how genuine he is.

Acknowledgments

As Bob and I [Clayton] put this book together, many people were mentioned who played various roles in the events, activities, and challenges of my life. Just as many things were omitted from the book, there are people who have played an important role in my life. Many of these people have not been mentioned in the text of this book, or are only briefly mentioned. While I can't fully account for everyone, I want to make partial amends. If your name is mentioned in the text, it won't be repeated here.

Any success I have enjoyed in the hospital business has, in large part, been through the talents of others. All of my years in the hospital industry had me working with so many people. To the medical staffs of Phoebe Putney Memorial Hospital; Sumter County Hospital; City-County Hospital in LaGrange, Georgia; Palmyra Park Hospital; and all the other hospitals that were part of HCA or HealthTrust: I know that it couldn't have been done without you. You supported me and taught me a lot about physician-administrator relations.

In Albany, Americus, and LaGrange, Georgia, there were many in the community who helped the hospitals and me personally. Sam Hunter, the Americus banker who helped the hospital manage its cash flow, Bob Ellington in Albany, and Fuller Calloway in LaGrange should be singled out.

The staffs of HealthTrust and HCA's corporate offices included thousands of dedicated and hard-working people. A few have been part of the stories told in this book and the roster of HTI employees listed in the appendix. A couple of people who slipped through the cracks include Andrew (Woody) Miller, John Colton, George Mercy, Helen King Cummings, Phil Patton, Shirley Newton, David Vanderwater, and Bob Yeager.

The staffs of the community agencies, professional associations, and corporations whose boards I was fortunate enough to serve on helped me so much in fulfilling the community service roles I have played. Let me mention: Tom Corts, president, and Joe Dean, dean of the Pharmacy School at Samford University; Bill Trout, president, Rhodes College; Bob Fisher, president, Belmont University; Joe Johnson, former president of University of Tennessee; Margaret Perry, former president of University of Tennessee, Martin; Mike Bromberg, Cam Thompson, and Tom Sculley, all had been involved with the Federation of American Health Systems; Dick Davidson, American Hospital Association; Martha Ingram, CEO of Ingram Industries; John Clay, CEO of SunTrust Bank, Tennessee; and Zygmunt Nagorski, Aspen Institute.

I have been fortunate to have made friends because of my involvement with the political process, especially in Tennessee. This allows me to call many people friends and mentors. The list includes: Ned Ray McWherter, former governor of Tennessee; Jimmy Naifeh, speaker of the house, Tennessee Legislature; the late Shelby Rhinehart, former Tennessee state legislator; John Bragg, former Tennessee state legislator; Harlan Mathews, Tennessee state senator; Matt Kisber, Tennessee state senator and current Tennessee commissioner of economic development; Cleve Smith, political consultant; Ray Bell, contractor; and Carl Johnson (former commissioner of transportation who also helped me start LifeTrust).

Close friends can generally be counted on one hand. I have been blessed because I need both hands and some of my toes. A few who have been there "through thick and thin" are: Charlie Mann, John Haley, Tom Raney, Tom Foster, Aubrey Harwell, Gordon Inman, Rudy Ruark, and Parker Sherrill.

When I came out of the locker room for the second half, my team was smaller, but no less important to me. A few of those people not mentioned in the text include: Bill Cook, Chris Kyriopoulous, Mike Murphy, Joan Rubicon, Diane Turman, Nancy Allen, and Mark Vandiver.

For anyone who is not mentioned in the text or above, but feels they should have been, I apologize.

Clayton McWhorter
Nashville, Tennessee
Spring 2003

HEALTHTRUST, INC. THE HOSPITAL COMPANY

The following individuals constituted the founding corporate team of HealthTrust, Inc., as of September 17, 1987.

R. Clayton McWhorter
Charles N. Martin, Jr.
Donald S. MacNaughton
Bud Adams
Michelle Diehm
Anita James
Cathy Repass
Richard Anderson
Ken Donahey
Russell Jenkins
Hector Rivas
Nevel Andrews
Michael Dumont
Milton Johnson
David Roberson
Ann Ayars
Mark Eddy
Tom Johnson
Arlene Robertson
Leota Barger
Linda Ellingwood
Ruby Jordan
Anita Roche
Vickie Beard
Teresa Ellis
James June
Keith Rye
William Bellet
Michael Ernst

Dale Kennedy
Jean Schweinhart
Martha Bennett
George Evans
Mike Koban
Beville Searcy
Vince Booker
Esther Fair
Jodi Kravitz
David Smith
Linda Boyd
Cindy Florou
Lisa Lakin
Ron Spaeth
Steve Brandt
Richard Francis
David Lassiter
Kathy Spears
Dianne Brown
Rod Gallimore
Jeri Ann Latham
Patricia Spond
Terry Bryant
Barbara Garvin
Lance Lott
Don Street
Jean Buckner
Richard Gaston
Kelly Styles

Betty Bumbalough
John Geer
Jim Main
Brenda Taylor
Larry Burkhart
Carl George
Karen Thacker
Jimmie Carol Byers
David Gragg
John McCaslin
Betty Triplett
Beth Campbell
Faye Gray
Robert McKelvey
Andrea Vietta
Ellen Carroll
Loraine Gray
Stuart Voelpel
Brenda Ceruzzi
Jim Hahn
Randolph Millard
Bob Vraciu
Yonnie Chesley
Bill Haire
Linda Miller
Bob Wallace
Zachary Clayton
Dan Hall
Deborah Miller
Judy Ware
Susan Clifford
Marianne Hamilton
Mac Moore
Mark Warren
Debra Coleman
Diane Hardick

Terry Moran
Steve Whitmore
Erin Collins
Melvin Harris
Tom Neill
Patricia Wilkerson
Mary Kay Conlon
Connie Hill
Norman Nichols
Robert Will
Hud Connery
Tim Hill
Richard Parker
Alice Williams
Kay Cox
Regie Hines
Ken Perry
Herb Williams
Walter Cramer
Leon Hooper
Kimmyth Pesz
Frank Williams
Pam Crawford
Robert Hornachek
Jack Porter
Drusilla Wright
Jim Dalton
Jerry Hussey
Sandy Poteet
David Young
Glenn Davis
John Hyde
Diane Poyner
Carl Denny
Debbie Jacobs
Ann Price

Index